Advance praise for
The Art of Startups

"This book is a must-read for every founder."
—Dan Lyons, Author of *Disrupted: My Misadventure in the Startup Bubble*

"The enduring brilliance of Machiavelli is brought to life in this very compelling and very accessible book. A must-read for every entrepreneur and corporate strategist!"
—Mark DeSantis, CEO, Bloomfield Robotics, and Adjunct Professor of Entrepreneurship, Carnegie Mellon University

"Insightful, accessible and fun. If readers enjoyed *The Lean Startup* and *Zero to One* they are going to love *The Art of Startups*. The author has done a great job to educate its readers in a very clever and entertaining way!"
—Spandana Nakka, Co-founder and CEO, Sleek

"A startup guide like no other. Tech breakthroughs have washed ashore legions of spirited entrepreneurs; Edoardo Maggini hands them a tool to survive and thrive."
—Igor Pejic, Author of *Blockchain Babel: The Crypto Craze and the Challenge to Business*

"*The Art of Startups* is an incredible read, easy and relatable and yet full of condensed structure and insights. It's a great guide bringing together all of the stages of startup entrepreneurship, with a strong emphasis on strategy and approaches. I wish I had something like this to guide me when I started my first company in 2008!"
—Max Gurvits, VC, Vitosha Venture Partners; Co-founder and Chief Host at SummitSummit

"A brilliant and wonderfully entertaining book. An unstoppable read, full of surprises and rich with insight for every entrepreneur—first time or seasoned."
—Avery J. Lu, Co-founder, Chief Marketing Officer and Managing Director, Investments, ActionSpot Startup Studio

"*The Art of Startups* really brings to life that behind great startups, and indeed great products in general, are great people. Telling the stories of these people is important in order to learn how to not only develop successful startups but also apply startup smarts inside corporate organizations."

—Tim Heard, Co-founder and MD, Circle of Intrapreneurs

"While startups and entrepreneurship are inherently about invention, some of the best lessons in business can come from looking in the past to shape the future. Edoardo Maggini has done just that with *The Art of Startups* as he applies the principles of Machiavelli to winning in today's modern world of entrepreneurship."

—Dave Knox, Marketing Executive Coach, Venture Investor and Author of *Predicting the Turn: The High Stakes Game of Business between Startups and Blue Chips*

"Modern leaders need to challenge themselves with divergent thinking in order to stay sharp. *The Art of Startups* is a great opportunity to reacquaint yourself with tried and true business principles in a fresh new context."

—Michael Ventura, CEO, Sub Rosa, and Author of *Applied Empathy*

"Part business strategy book, part leadership development book and 100% graphic novel, *The Art of Startups* is an entertaining guide to business innovation."

—Nir Eyal, Bestselling Author of *Hooked and Indistractable*

The Art of Startups

How to Beat Larger Companies Using Machiavelli's War Strategies

Edoardo Maggini

A Business Graphic Novel

Best Business Book Proposal of the Year

Shortlisted for the Financial Times Bracken Bower Prize 2018 as Best Business Book of the Year

Edoardo Maggini, serial entrepreneur and inventor

ANTHEM PRESS

Anthem Press
An imprint of Wimbledon Publishing Company
www.anthempress.com

This edition first published in UK and USA 2020
by ANTHEM PRESS
75–76 Blackfriars Road, London SE1 8HA, UK
or PO Box 9779, London SW19 7ZG, UK
and
244 Madison Ave #116, New York, NY 10016, USA

British Library Cataloguing-in-Publication Data
A catalogue record for this book is available from the British Library.

Library of Congress Cataloging-in-Publication Data
Library of Congress Control Number: 2019955628

ISBN-13: 978-1-78527-168-7 (Hbk)
ISBN-10: 1-78527-168-7 (Hbk)

This title is also available as an e-book.

CONTENTS

INTRODUCTION BY THE AUTHOR

Startup Landscape

Startups are increasingly becoming the engine of innovation across all industries. We are living in an age where an entire generation of young entrepreneurs with different backgrounds and skill sets is coming together and collaborating with a desire to disrupt existing markets, challenge the status quo, replace the old with the new and, above all else, make the world a better place. Startups are constantly facing the challenge of how to make an impact given their initial small size and limited resources. Those few that do manage to survive can quickly find themselves swamped in the oversaturated market, unable to make any decent progress.

According to the U.S. Small Business Administration, 89.6 percent of companies are small businesses (fewer than 20 employees) and they account for more than half of the total workforce. Over 627,000 new companies open their doors each year; however, more than 50 percent do not reach past the five-year mark. So, how can they establish themselves among their immediate competitors, let alone defeat larger, more established companies? Is the story of David and Goliath still relevant in the modern business world?

When I was studying for my MBA, I have always felt that most of the strategies taught were geared for large organizations already well established such as corporations or multinational companies. However, talking about merge and acquisition, international expansions and vertical integrations in the context of new ventures, it is very unrealistic. Not much was said on how small organizations can breakthrough. Actually, trying to apply large companies' strategies to small startups will result most of the time into a loss of focus if not into a catastrophe.

Hence the need to write an engaging book that offers unique, viable solutions to all the problems that small startups face especially in their early stages.

This book provides practical teachings on how startup founders can strengthen their foundations, how to reach the pinnacle of the business world and ultimately how anyone can become a virtuous leader of a startup in the model of *The Prince*.

Why Machiavelli?

What does a 500-year-old figure from history have to do with the world of startups? I first encountered Machiavelli in high school in Italy. At the time, he didn't represent much more to me than just another part of my studies, but he came rushing back when I moved to the United States to finish high school in a small town of Ohio. I used to talk to people who knew little about Italy, but who could still quote Machiavelli's most famous lines: "The end justifies the means" and "It is better to be feared than loved."

Machiavelli seemed to be even more popular in America than in Italy. This triggered my curiosity and pushed me to do more research on him, and I realized that throughout history, politicians, generals, sports coaches and other leaders have all harnessed his principles in their various fields. He has also been criticized as being overly cynical, cruel or cutthroat. However, I think this is too dismissive and partial. Machiavelli was, more than anything, a pragmatic realist. He devoted himself to finding patterns in human nature and history, and was perfectly aware of what was ethical and unethical, encouraging aspiring leaders to reach their goals by "Virtue"; to rely on hard work rather than luck; and to try to be loved rather than be feared (while noting it's easier to be feared). He also understood that necessity and emergency compels leaders to make controversial decisions.

During my studies at Harvard Business School, I began to apply Machiavelli's principles to the business world, finding his teachings tremendously modern and useful for my own startup. I realized that as, a serial entrepreneur, I was already applying many of his tactics without even being aware of it. So, I started decoding and adapting his writings to the world of startups, testing his teachings in the field.

From this experience, and from Machiavelli's two most influential books, *The Art of War* and *The Prince*, came the idea for *The Art of Startups*.

Book Structure

The Art of Startups follows Lorenzo, an ambitious entrepreneur. FESTINA LENTE, his startup, is going through difficult times due to scarce resources and fierce competition from bigger companies. But thanks to Machiavelli's principles and strategies, Lorenzo and his team are able to shift gear and grow into an influential company, eventually beating out their everlasting rival AUT CAESAR.

I have chosen the comic-book format for the following reasons:

1. No business book about startups has ever been treated as graphic novel, making *The Art of Startups* completely unique and groundbreaking.

2. All discussions or studies of Machiavelli have been exclusively treated in traditional ways, that is, through text or lecture formats, and it's my intention to create a fresh, fun and more accessible format that is perfectly suited for the psychographics of most startup communities.

3. Storytelling methods of dialogue and plot complete with illustrations and general gamification will both aid learning and application of our subject matter.

The book is broken up in five chapters:

Chapter 1: "Maneuvers," outlines four distinctive strategies that a small startup can utilize in order to gain the upper hand against bigger companies.

Chapter 2: "Innovation," dives deep into the world of innovation and teaches how to innovate with limited available resources.

Chapter 3: "Alliances," focuses on the usefulness of alliances in order to spur the growth of a startup and how to negotiate the best deals.

Chapter 4: "Leadership," delves into what it means to be a good leader in terms of traits, psychology and social interactions.

Bonus Chapter: Miscellaneous tools and tactics that have proved useful in startups.

At the end of every chapter, the reader will find schematics summaries to recap and make sure nothing is lost in the illustrations. Furthermore, the reader will find real case studies of other startups that will facilitate the application of the business teachings.

FOREWORD

When *The Art of Startups* crossed my desk I was curious and thrilled to pick it up. It's not every day you see a business book presented as a graphic novel.

Technology is all about innovation, creating inventive solutions to existing problems. Edoardo Maggini has created a true innovation with this book, tackling the difficulties of founding and growing a startup in a totally unique way. He's done what any good entrepreneur should in this competitive world: creatively break down paradigms and build a new structure from it all.

The Art of Startups reflects this entrepreneurial spirit, developing and exploring specific strategies and principles useful to both the fresh and more-seasoned startuppers.

Although serious in subject-matter, its storytelling style, harking back to old mangas, makes it easy to digest and incredibly fun to read. Having studied both industrial and graphic design, I really appreciated the quality of visuals as a means to deliver information.

Starting a business is obviously not a walk in the park. It's a maze filled with traps and wolves, to borrow from Machiavelli. The Art of Startups can definitely help you along the way and I hope it will inspire a new wave of founders around the world to start their own ventures. I know I'll be carrying a copy with me as I continue my own journey.

Joe Gebbia, Airbnb Co-founder

CAST OF CHARACTERS

FABRIZIO:
THE RIGHT-HAND MAN OF LORENZO. AN IVY LEAGUE GRADUATE WITH AN IQ OF OVER 140 WHO WORKED AT THE FOREMOST STARTUP AUT CAESAR. QUICKLY GROWING DISILLUSIONED AT AUT CAESAR, HE QUIT TO HELP IMPLEMENT LORENZO'S VISION.

COSIMA:
A PROGRAMMING GEEK WHO DOESN'T TALK OFTEN, BUT WHEN SHE DOES, SHE ALWAYS SAYS THE RIGHT THING. SHE IS FULLY COMMITTED TO FESTINA LENTE, AND WORKS 25/7.

LORENZO:
THE CEO OF FESTINA LENTE. A VISIONARY ENTREPRENEUR WITH TWO FAILED STARTUPS UNDER HIS BELT AND THE BELIEF THAT HIS THIRD ATTEMPT WILL BE SUCCESSFUL. A CONFIDENT, GOOD-LOOKING, AND CHARISMATIC MAN SEARCHING FOR THE THE RIGHT INGREDIENTS NEEDED TO BE A GREAT LEADER.

LUCREZIA: AN ATTRACTIVE, ASSERTIVE, AND INTUITIVE WOMAN WITH A BACKGROUND IN MARKETING AND SALES. SHE HAS GREAT BUSINESS ACUMEN, AND IS ALWAYS INCLINED TO BREAK THE RULES.

ALESSANDRO: THE INTERN AT FESTINA LENTE. HE IS FRESH OUT OF COLLEGE AND DOESN'T HAVE MUCH REAL-WORLD EXPERIENCE. HE CAN THEREFORE BE SOMEWHAT NAÏVE. BUT HE IS A FAST-LEARNER, AMBITIOUS, AND LORENZO HAS GREAT BELIEF IN HIS POTENTIAL.

ROBERTO VALTURIO: THE CURIOUS AND CRAFTY COMPUTER ENGINEER WHO JOINS FESTINA LENTE.

CLAYTON: AN EXPERIENCED INVESTMENT FUND MANAGER

BEATRICE: ONE OF LORENZO'S GOOD FRIENDS AND OWNER OF A STRUGGLING FOOD TRUCK BUSINESS

AUT CAESAR: THE DOMINANT COMPANY FOR A LONG TIME. FESTINA LENTE'S RIVAL

Chapter 1

MANEUVERS: HOW WEAK COMPANIES CAN OUTMANEUVER STRONGER ONES

This chapter outlines four distinctive strategies that a small startup can utilize in order to gain the upper hand against bigger companies:

- Innovation
- Concentration
- Acceleration
- Segmentation

EVEN WORSE: THE BIG COMPANIES ARE ONLY GETTING BIGGER AND IT'S NOT LOOKING LIKELY WE'LL GET CLOSE TO THEM ANYTIME SOON

ESPECIALLY **AUT CAESAR**. IT SEEMS LIKE THEY'VE BEEN AT THE TOP FOREVER, AND WILL BE FOR ETERNITY

WE ALL KNOW ABOUT YOUR DARK HISTORY **AUT CAESAR**, BUT THEIR FOUNDERS ARE *LEGENDS*

THEY'RE REALLY NOT THAT *LEGENDARY OR COOL*

BUT THEY'VE BEEN IN THE GAME SINCE THE BEGINNING, SINCE STARTUPS FIRST STARTED, SINCE BEFORE YOU AND I WERE BORN

AT LEAST, SINCE ALESSANDRO WAS BORN

I'M ONLY THREE YEARS YOUNGER THAN YOU

EXACTLY, AND HENCE I'M THREE YEARS WISER THAN YOU

THE
DAY AFTER...

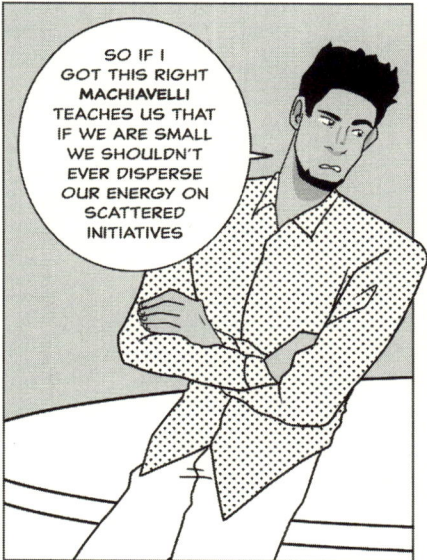

SO IF I GOT THIS RIGHT MACHIAVELLI TEACHES US THAT IF WE ARE SMALL WE SHOULDN'T EVER DISPERSE OUR ENERGY ON SCATTERED INITIATIVES

OUR ONLY CHANCE IS TO USE ALL OUR STRENGTH TO STRIKE THE WEAKEST POINT OF OUR RIVAL

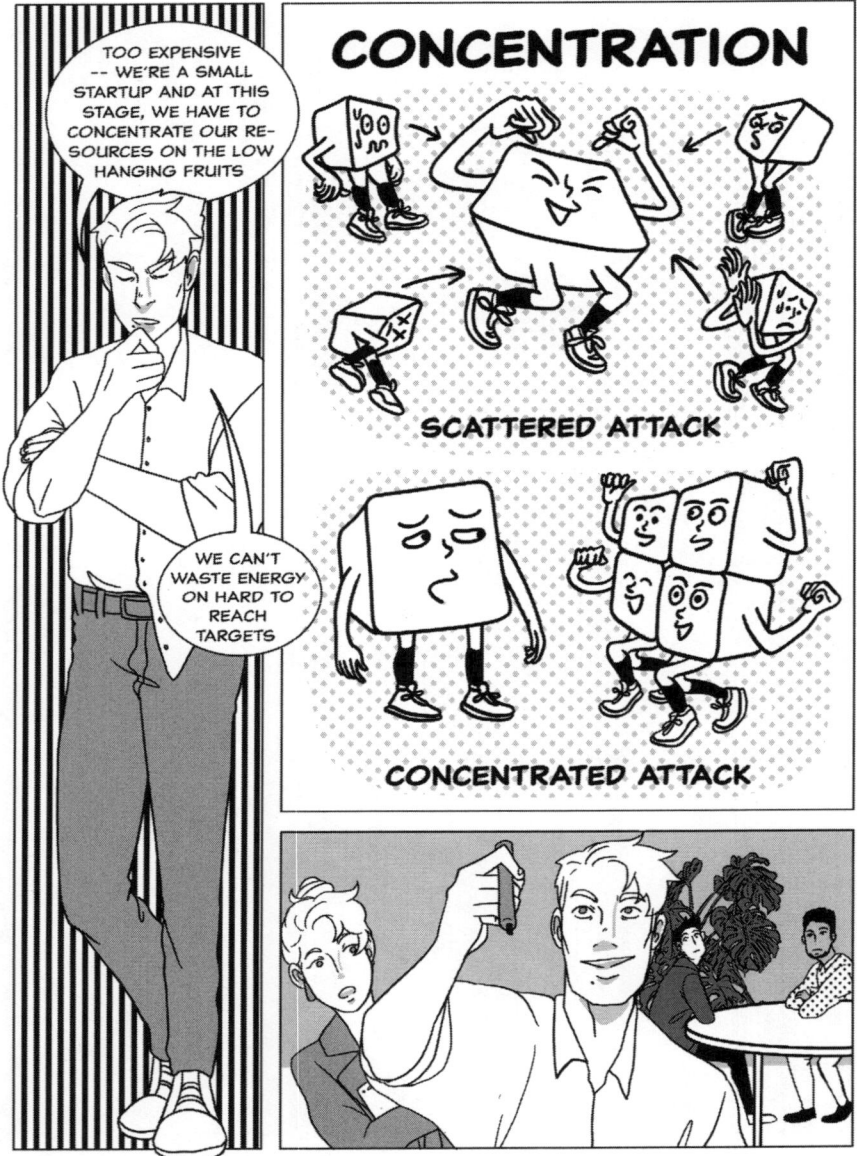

ASSUMING THAT WE HAVE A TOTAL OF 10 CANNONBALLS (IN A STARTUP CONTEXT THE 10 CANNONBALLS COULD REPRESENT $10K OF YOUR BUDGET). BY SPREADING THE 10 BULLETS EVENLY AMONG THE CANNONS, ONLY 2 BULLETS WILL HIT THE TARGET

0.3
0.9
0.6
0.8
0.4

SCATTERED SCENARIO
(0.9X2+0.3X2+0.6X2+0.4X2+0.9X2)/
(0.9+0.3+0.6+0.4+0.9)=2

BUT RATHER THAN DISPERSING OUR RESOURCES, IF WE COULD CONCENTRATE OUR ATTACK, AND FIRE ALL 10 CANNONBALLS USING ONLY THE TWO CANNONS WITH THE HIGHEST STRIKING COEFFICIENT, THEN WE'LL BE FAR MORE LETHAL

0.3
0.9
0.6
0.8
0.4

CONCENTRATED SCENARIO
(0.9X5+0.8X5)/(0.9+0.8)=5

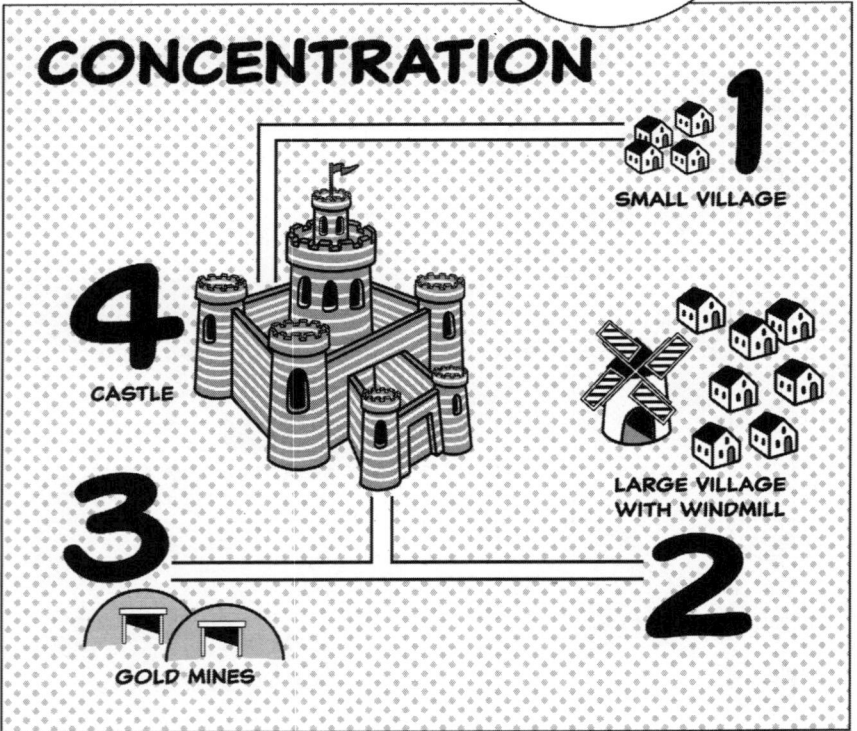

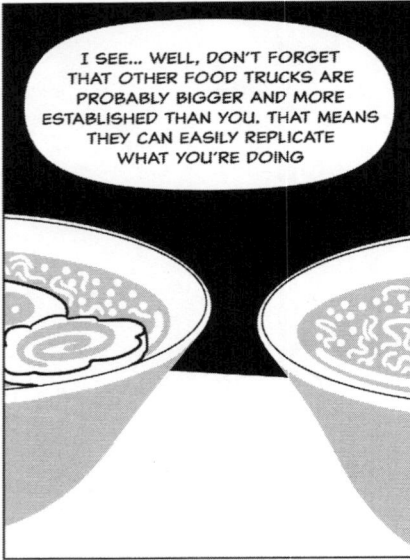

DON'T THINK I'D SPEND VALUABLE COMPANY ASSETS ON ENTERTAINING MY EMPLOYEES. WE'RE HERE TO STUDY, TO LEARN. SPORTS ARE LIKE WAR GAMES YOU SEE...

THE CLOSEST WE'LL GET TO WITNESSING A BATTLE, LIKE MACHIAVELLI MUST HAVE DONE.

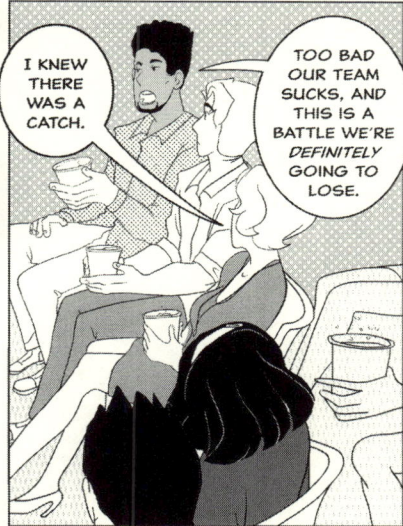

I KNEW THERE WAS A CATCH.

TOO BAD OUR TEAM SUCKS, AND THIS IS A BATTLE WE'RE *DEFINITELY* GOING TO LOSE.

ALWAYS THE OPTIMIST.

FABRIZIO IS RIGHT TO BE DISCOUR-AGED.

BASED ON THE ALGORITHM THAT I CREATED, WHICH TAKES INTO ACCOUNT PLAYER FORM, HISTORICAL HEAD-TO-HEAD RESULTS, AND HUMIDITY LEVELS, WE ACTUALLY HAVE AN 18.23% CHANCE OF WINNING.

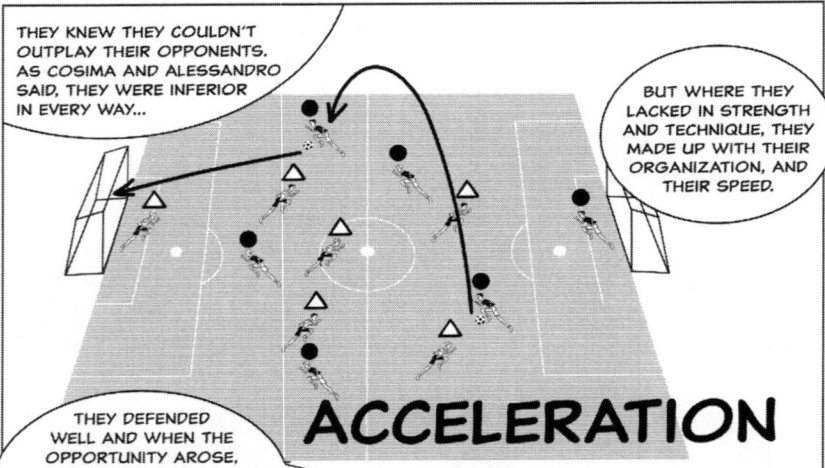

ACCELERATION

SEGMENTATION

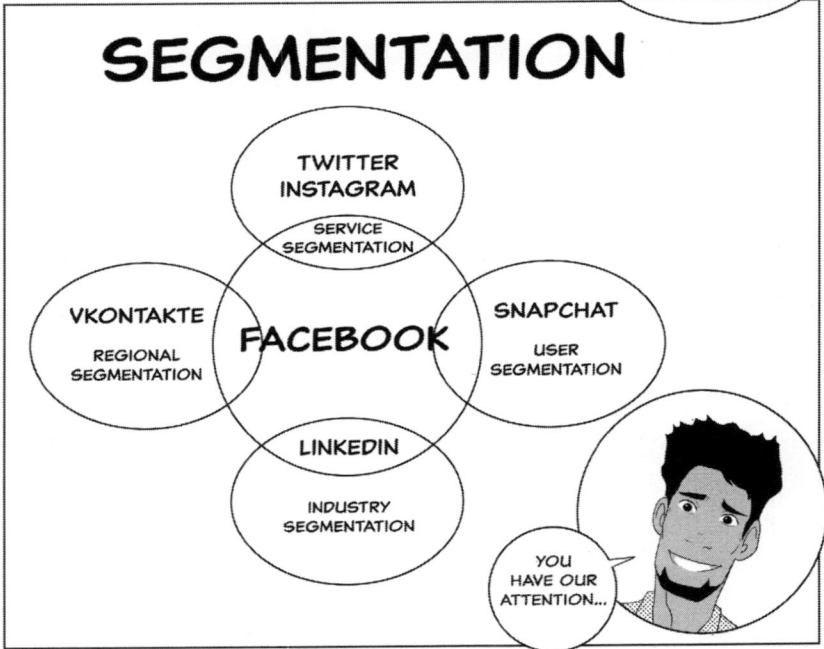

THERE ARE FOUR TYPES OF SEGMENTATION THAT WE CAN APPLY TO A BIGGER COMPETITOR'S BUSINESS:

1. **SERVICE SEGMENTATION:** SEGMENTING ONLY ONE SPECIFIC SERVICE THAT A COMPETITOR OFFERS AND SPECIALIZING IN IT

2. **USER SEGMENTATION:** IDENTIFYING A POCKET OF THE USER BASE AND TAILORING A SERVICE TO FIT SPECIFICALLY FOR THEM

3. **INDUSTRY SEGMENTATION:** SPINNING YOUR COMPETITOR'S SERVICE FOR A DIFFERENT INDUSTRY

4. **GEOGRAPHICAL SEGMENTATION:** CUSTOMIZING THE SERVICE FOR USERS OF A DIFFERENT GEOGRAPHICAL AREA

Chapter 1: Maneuvers

Innovation

Without innovation, small startups would have no chance of winning battles against bigger companies. Quite simply because they can't afford to replicate what's already being done, and why would they want to? It's like challenging LeBron James to a slam dunk competition—a perfect recipe for failure. If you challenge him to something else on an entirely different battlefield—say skiing, chess or knitting—you'll have a much higher chance of victory.

Through innovation, by offering something new and different, startups can encourage users to leave their old providers and try something more in tune with them. This is critical for a startup's establishment and survival.

However, if the innovation is successful, bigger companies will likely try matching it. This means small startups have to be creative and flexible, and willing to take risks by constantly innovating their service or product. To do so, it's essential they keep as close as possible to their users. Direct contact with users will teach who they are and what they like/dislike. It will also allow them to monitor and anticipate their users' evolving needs.

Speaking of creativity, let's say your bigger opponent is running an ad campaign through traditional media. They can afford to dominate television, when you can't. So, you'll have to choose a different space to promote your product/service, such as through social media, as Cookie DO did, a small business that began selling e-commerce cookie dough. Two years and 78,000 Instagram followers later, it was time to open a real brick-and-mortar retail store in New York City. What do you think would have happened if they'd tried to take a more standard approach, such as first opening the retail store and then advertising on traditional media channels?

Startups can take various initiatives to get closer to their users. These include the following:

- Making the cofounders' faces visible (avoid hiding behind agencies, brokers, or third parties)
- Starting with a small batch of users
- Focusing first in an area of expertise or on a familiar user segment. Find success there, and then branch out

Concentration

During a battle, a small startup must never disperse its army. Instead, it should concentrate its few soldiers (manpower, money, technology, etc.) on a single point. Attack those targets that are within reach, at the periphery of the kingdom where it's easy, where it's easier to win some battles. Build a fort around each battleground, which represents the loyal user who promotes the service/product, and then proceed to the next objective.

If a startup instead invests its resources evenly among different initiatives and attacks different points, especially those not aligned with its strategy, there will never be a significant impact.

The loot from each individual battle may be modest at the beginning, but—by repeatedly concentrating attacks, winning small battles, and consolidating them—the small startup will start winning more fruitful battles, and can eventually win the war.

When deciding where to attack, consider the following possible blind spots of competitors:

- Overlooked regions (cultures, legal system, infrastructures, telecommunications, etc.).
- Small user niches, areas, or segments (e.g., dissatisfied users). The more specific these are, the higher chance of winning users from competitors.
- A single product or service, especially a competitor's flawed product or inefficient service—cofounders should make a choice based on what they are confident in, and what they think can be done better.

Keeping Machiavelli in mind, startups should hit their opponents as hard as possible to their Achilles' heel preventing a retaliation. In other words, the strength of each hit is far more important than how many hits it lands. A high number of hits with a low coefficient of accuracy or power will not yield the desired outcome, because each hit consumes time, energy and money. It will also reveal your strategy to rivals.

So let's say you decide to run a Google Ads campaign using your competitor's keywords, knowing this will boost your visibility among users interested in that type of service. This is a far better strategy than scattering your attacks with a general e-mail blast, or through cold calling and flyers.

Scenario 1—Concentrated Attack

Attacks	Striking Force Coefficient	No. of Attacks	Total Damage
Google Ads on competitor's page	0.6	1	
Reach out for dissatisfied competitor's users	0.8	1	0.7

Scenario 2—Scattered Attack

Attacks	Striking Force Coefficient	No. of Attacks	Total Damage
E-mail blast campaign	0.5	1	
Cold calling	0.6	1	
Flyers	0.1	1	0.35
Radio commercial	0.2	1	

As we can see, in Scenario 2, despite the greater amount of resources spent, we were able to inflict only a limited amount of damage to our opponent (by "damage" we mean users acquired). This is because everytime that we diversify our initiatives we decrease the penetration coefficient.

In Scenario 1, we carried out only two attacks but each with a very high striking power because we concentrated all our resources on targeting. This scenario is ideal attack for small startups, because remember: small armies have limited resources, which means accuracy is all the more important. So if a campaign is not yielding the expected result, cease it and refocus those resources on fewer but more impactful attacks.

The concentration strategy can be applied to overturn the odds of a battle in numerous different business scenarios. For instance, in marketing, focus your resources on those channels that yield the most results in terms of user acquisition. Or focus on social media channels that receive the most responses from viewers.

In terms of building your business identity, considering concentrating first on a designated area—group all your initiatives in that area in order to create critical mass. Once the area has been won, build outward to other neighborhoods or regions with similar conditions.

For example, In-n-Out Burger focused on becoming a food landmark in California, a must go-for visitors, before expanding to other neighborhood states.

A few more things to keep in mind:

- When investing resources, concentrate them first by taking care of loyal and paying users. Build yourself around them rather than chasing hard-to-catch fish.
- When networking, concentrate time with people you know, because they'll be more willing to help you. Additionally, approach investors within your reach, as they'll be more likely to pay attention
- When it comes to innovating, don't scatter your resources across different ideas—focus on the most value-adding ones. For example, consider Amazon in its early days. The company was very careful to concentrate all its efforts only and exclusively on books. After dominating the book space, they expanded horizontally, conquering all other categories.

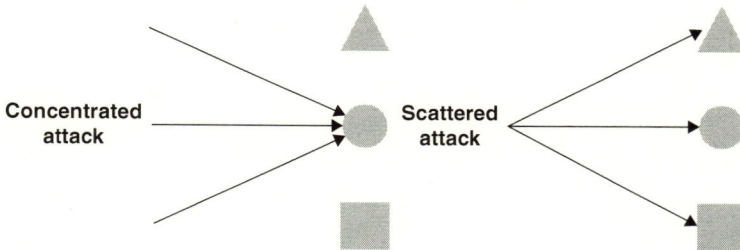

It all comes down to the Focal Point Principle:

All of your initiatives should converge on one clear and planned focal point. If they don't, you'll needlessly disperse energy and resources. Many startups pursue too many initiatives that are not strictly linked to their focal point, and they don't make significant progress because of it.

A Winning Startup

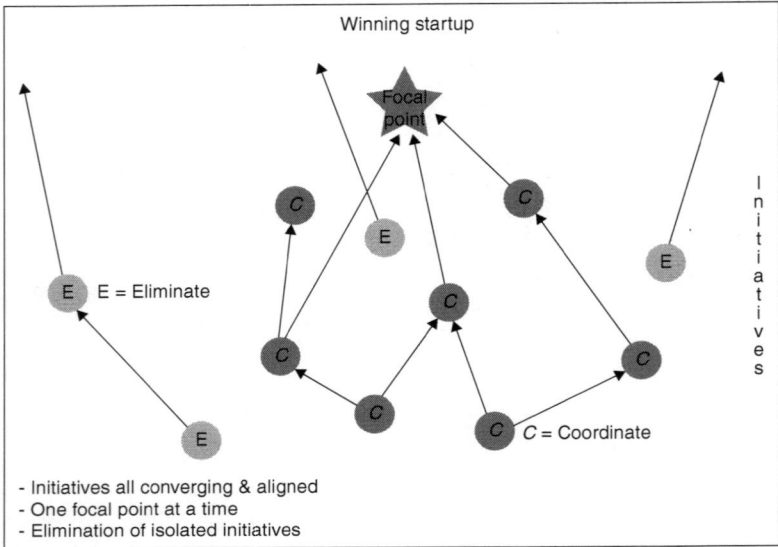

Winning startup

- Initiatives all converging & aligned
- One focal point at a time
- Elimination of isolated initiatives

- Initiatives are aligned and converge
- One focal point at a time
- Elimination of isolated initiatives

A Losing Startup

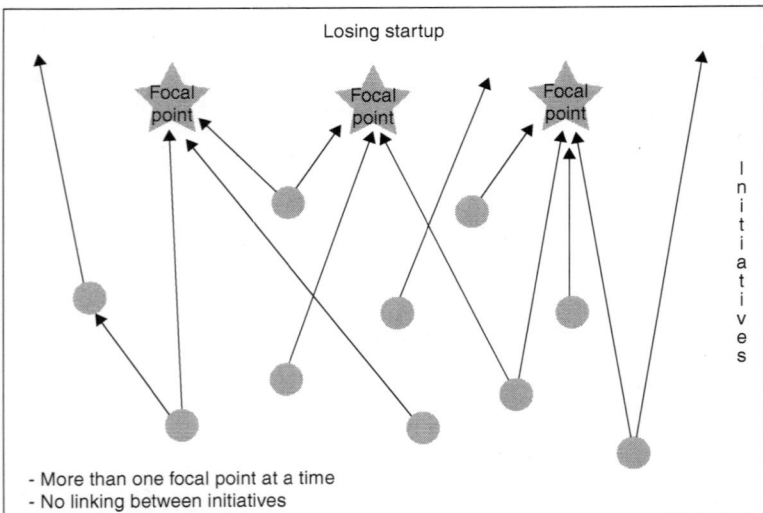

Losing startup

- More than one focal point at a time
- No linking between initiatives

- More than one focal point
- No link between initiatives

For a newly launched startup, the good news is that it's not impossible to erode the market share of established companies—if you take the right steps. As usual, as the first mover, established companies have a higher degree of inefficiency. As it grows in size, its blind spots increase, and it tends to stop innovating, even if this means losing touch with niches of clients, and leaving some users unhappy.

Acceleration

It's actually quite simple: if your opponent is bigger and stronger, you need to be faster. History is full of examples where the weaker army was able to win using its speed. Consider the American Revolution, where the incursions of small and agile American troops were able to defeat the much larger and more powerful but stiff British army.

In business, it's always more evident that it's not the big that eat the small but it's the fast that eat the slow. Speed is a critical competitive advantage for startups.

Big companies are notoriously slow, especially when it comes to decision making and to execution. So acceleration is fundamental when it comes to outmaneuvering them. Plus, the momentum generated by accelerating boosts the morale of a small startup, making it more attractive to investors and those looking for a company to join forces with.

Sports—arguably warfare translated to an athletic spectacle—gives plenty of other great example of acceleration. But let's take a look at one tactic in particular in soccer: the "Counterattack," which is often used by weaker teams when facing stronger ones.

Basically, the weaker team, forced to go on the defensive most of the game, tries to quickly win the ball and with a long launch bypassing their opponent's midfield line. They then use players known for their speed known as wings to latch onto the ball and create a goal-scoring opportunity. This simple one-two punch utilizes nothing other than acceleration and surprise.

In the world of startups, Facebook's motto is "Go fast and break things." They know that fast execution is far more effective than perfect execution, because no one knows if something new will work until it's tried. So, by accelerating their execution, startups can spur their innovations and reduce errors by more quickly understanding what works and what doesn't.

The success of Rocket Internet best epitomizes this:

Founded in 2007 by three German brothers (Marc, Oliver and Alexander Samwer), Rocket Internet and its portfolio companies employ more than

30,000 people. It has a market cap north of $3 billion, which at times has risen above $6 billion.

Rocket Internet's early business strategy was simple: take inspiration from Silicon Valley startups; make copycats of them adapted to local markets in Europe, South America and Asia; and then grow them at lightning speeds. Once the local market was dominated, it sold the copycat to the company that inspired it.

The Samwer brothers started CityDeals in 2010 and sold it to Groupon for $170 million just five months later. They also started Alando and sold it to eBay for $38 million within 100 days of launching the site.

Because they didn't take funding for Alando, they created shockwaves by how quickly they grew. As one employee said, "Once we pick which startup we want to replicate, the next step is all about growth. Fast growth at all costs. The first six months is 100% week-over-week growth. Then, after $1 million in revenue, it's 20% growth every month. We built billion-dollar companies in less than 36 months."

Three factors made the Rocket Internet business model successful:

• Expanding the geography of the service or product and concentrating on that location
• A better understanding of users' needs in those markets (such as product offerings or purchasing power)
• Accelerated execution to the speed of light

The Myth of Multitasking

Accelerating shouldn't be confused with multitasking. Even if we are encouraged to multitask by our boss, peers, or clients, it's a myth. It's scientifically proven that the human brain is not designed for it, and it always results in a loss of efficiency. Taking on more than one task at a time means sloppy execution, which slows down our operations and depletes a huge amount of energy. Also, multitasking involved too much decision making. In short: it's not sustainable.

So again, keep in mind concentration—startuppers should always concentrate on one task at a time, tackle it, and then move on to the next as fast as possible. Move fast, learn fast, and you'll find yourself perfecting your executions as a natural consequence of trial and error.

To accelerate, it's also important to have beforehand a clear idea in mind what the next task will be, and plan two or three steps ahead. Otherwise, you'll find yourself slowing down. We can think of this as linear execution.

(A) Efficient Linear Execution

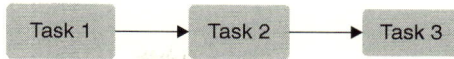

(B) Inefficient Multitask Execution

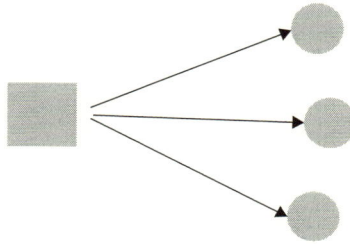

Segmentation—"Divide and Conquer"

When facing an army much bigger and stronger, the only way to have a chance of victory is to breaking it up into smaller parts more manageable to our size. In that way defeating one part after another we will eventually win the war.

Segmentation in the startup context means breaking up large chunks of value from bigger companies into more manageable pieces. This can be applied to four areas of the value chain. Let's look at each in the context of Facebook as the dominating company, which was broken up by smaller startups as challenger companies.

(1) Regional segmentation

 VKontakte → The most popular social media site in Russia. It's essentially Facebook customized for Russian users.

(2) Service/Product segmentation

 → **Segmented** the comments feature of Facebook and specialized in it, becoming the go-to platform for sharing ideas and comments.

 → **Segmented** the photo-sharing feature of Facebook and focused on becoming the best photo-sharing channel.

(3) User segmentation

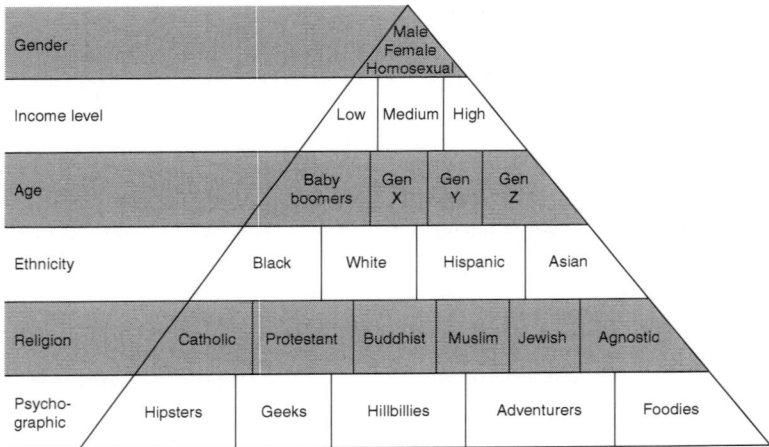

 → **Segmented** Facebook's photo-sharing feature and retargeted on a specific demographic of Facebook users, that is, millennials/teenagers (those with the highest usage of social media).

(4) Industry segmentation

 → **Segmented** Facebook's general concept and applied it to the business professionals industry.

Another very successful case of segmentation was carried out by Grindr to the detriment of Tinder. Within the large Tinder user base, Grindr segmented by targeting the homosexual user base.

Here are some more examples of users segmentation, but you can segment anything you think best suits your goals (geography, products, service, etc.):

Segmentation:

Gender					Male Female Homosexual			
Income level				Low	Medium	High		
Age				Baby boomers	Gen X	Gen Y	Gen Z	
Ethnicity			Black	White		Hispanic	Asian	
Religion		Catholic	Protestant	Buddhist	Muslim	Jewish	Agnostic	
Psycho-graphic	Hipsters	Geeks	Hillbillies		Adventurers		Foodies	

Some Final Thoughts

A common mistake many startups make is to emulate the strategies of stronger companies. For example, trying to offer the same or similar products for as many users as possible. This always results in the unnecessary dispersion of force, and makes winning a battle very difficult (see concentration above). It's very important to prioritize your scarce resources, which makes segmentation an essential strategy and accelerate your execution at lighting speed.

When choosing in which segment to fight your battle:

- Look for areas with market inefficiencies. If a competitor offers 10 different products/services, choose only one and specialize in it. How small should your area be? That depends on how weak you are. The weaker you are, the smaller your area. Once you win it over, you can then expand geometric-ally: 2, 4, 8, 16, etc.
- Don't be afraid to do battle against bigger and established companies. Innovative companies have the ability to disrupt monopolies. Moreover, it's very likely for monopolies to overlook the fringes of their kingdom, such as unhappy customers and lack of innovation in their products and services. For small startups, that creates an ideal battlefield where victory can be assured by changing the rules of the game through innovation, concentration, segmentation and acceleration.
- Remember that areas with many competing companies are tough to break into, as most of the customer base is already segmented. In addition, any successful innovation will soon be matched, reducing a small startup's competitive advantage. However, startups can still apply the key maneuvers discussed more aggressively to create space in the market.

Segmentation Case Study: The Battle of Trafalgar

In 1805, at the end of the Napoleonic Wars, the British fleet found itself up against a combined French-Spanish fleet. The odds were stacked against the British, who only had 27 warships against 33.

Realizing they couldn't meet the enemy head-on, the British admiral Nelson went against conventional tactics. He took an innovative approach and divided his fleet in half, attacking the enemy's rear and center. This meant the enemy's front-most ships couldn't take part in the first engagement, so all 27 British ships fought against only 20–21 enemy ships, evening the odds. After winning the first engagement, Nelson attacked the remaining ships. The outcome was decisive for him: none of his ships were lost, whereas he sunk 22 enemy ships, and 11 fled.

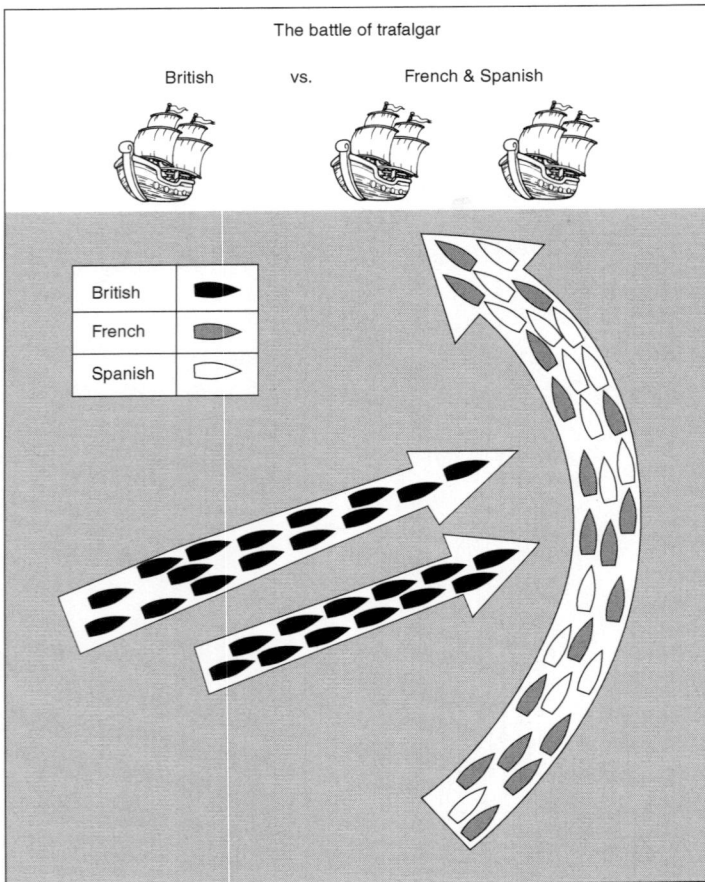

The battle of trafalgar

British   vs.   French & Spanish

British
French
Spanish

Chapter 2

INNOVATION: USING FEW RESOURCES TO INNOVATE IN A BIG WAY

"Whosoever desires constant success must innovate his conduct with the times."
Niccolo Machiavelli

This chapter dives deep into the world of innovation and teaches how to innovate with limited available resources by focusing on four distinct approaches to innovation that any startup can easily harness in order to innovate, namely,

- Entrepreneurial innovations: thinking more like an entrepreneur and less like an inventor, that is, taking advantage of unutilized technologies and finding ways to apply them to the market
- Problem-solving innovations: finding bottlenecks or inefficiencies in the market and attempting to solve them
- Failed innovations: understanding why previous innovations failed and picking it up from there
- Pivotal innovations: how to adapt to a more successful business model

THERE ARE FOUR TYPES OF INNOVATIONS THAT WE CAN HARNESS...

1. ENTREPRENEURIAL INNOVATIONS: APPLYING EXISTING TECHNOLOGY TO YOUR BUSINESS MODEL.

2. PROBLEM-SOLVING INNOVATIONS: MANY GREAT INNOVATIONS COME FROM SOLVING PROBLEMS.

3. FAILED INNOVATIONS: IMPROVING FAILED INNOVATIONS BY UNDERSTANDING WHY THEY FAILED.

4. PIVOTAL INNOVATIONS: YOU'VE GOT TO TEST, TEST, AND KEEP TESTING YOUR IDEA ON USERS AND BE OPEN TO PIVOTING AND CHANGING YOUR IDEA BASED ON THE RESULTS. YOU MIGHT FIND THE UNEXPECTED OUTCOME YOU WERE LOOKING FOR ALL ALONG.

HMM... VIAGRA WAS BORN OUT OF A PIVOTAL INNOVATION.

WHAT DO YOU MEAN ALESSANDRO?

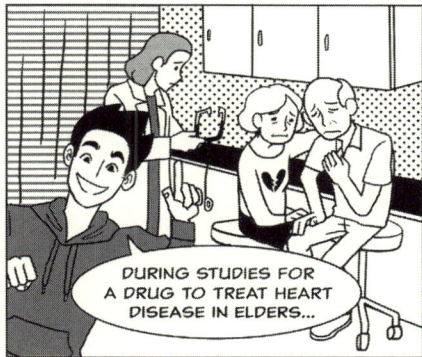

DURING STUDIES FOR A DRUG TO TREAT HEART DISEASE IN ELDERS...

DOCTORS GOT A COMPLETELY DIFFERENT OUTCOME IN MALE PATIENTS THAN EXPECTED... AND THAT'S HOW VIAGRA GOT INVENTED.

OH! YEAH

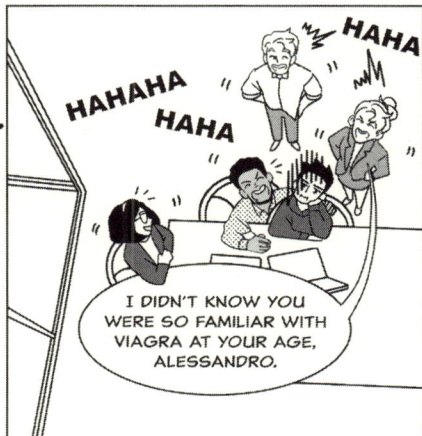

HAHA

HAHAHA HAHA

I DIDN'T KNOW YOU WERE SO FAMILIAR WITH VIAGRA AT YOUR AGE, ALESSANDRO.

A COUPLE OF WEEKS LATER

HEY FABRIZIO, HOW'S THE NEW PROJECT MANAGEMENT SOFTWARE?

COSIMA WAS SAYING IT'S THE LATEST IN THE MARKET.

A LOT OF THE TOOLS ARE JUST NOT THAT USEFUL FOR US, AND JUST MANAGE TO SLOW US DOWN. PLUS WITH THE LEARNING CURVE TO MASTER IT...

IT'S ALMOST A WASTE OF TIME.

THE OLD SOFTWARE WAS ACTUALLY MUCH BETTER. EASY, LEAN, FAST, STRAIGHT TO THE POINT.

IT'S DEFINITELY STATE OF THE ART. BUT TO BE HONEST, IT'S TOO FLASHY.

WHAT DO YOU MEAN?

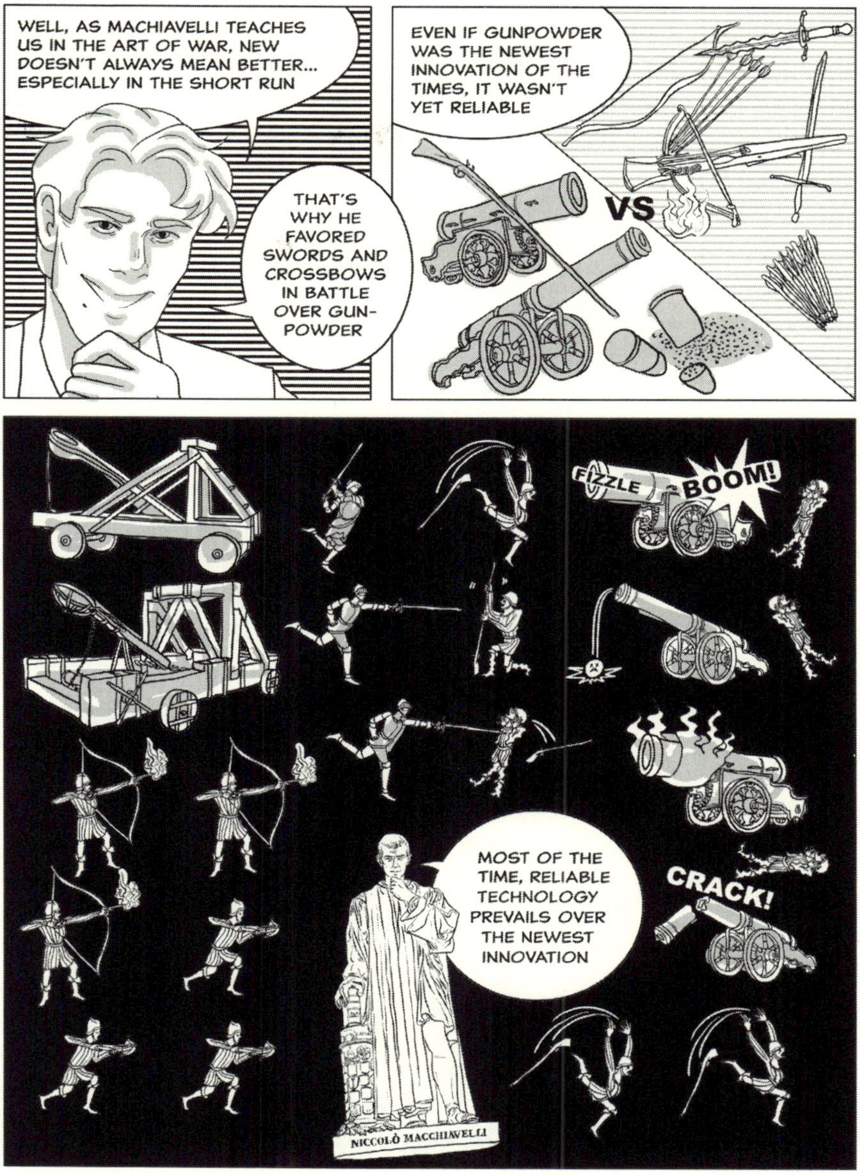
WELL, AS MACHIAVELLI TEACHES US IN THE ART OF WAR, NEW DOESN'T ALWAYS MEAN BETTER... ESPECIALLY IN THE SHORT RUN
THAT'S WHY HE FAVORED SWORDS AND CROSSBOWS IN BATTLE OVER GUN-POWDER
EVEN IF GUNPOWDER WAS THE NEWEST INNOVATION OF THE TIMES, IT WASN'T YET RELIABLE
VS
FIZZLE
BOOM!
MOST OF THE TIME, RELIABLE TECHNOLOGY PREVAILS OVER THE NEWEST INNOVATION
CRACK!
NICCOLÒ MACCHIAVELLI

Chapter 2: Innovation

For the most part, human evolution is characterized by two types of innovations: **incremental innovation** and **radical** (or breakthrough) **innovation**.

Incremental innovation means building on what already exists, and is usually sparked by necessity. Its constant improvement and problem-solving it's carry out by a variety of different people and players. Think for a second about communications. People have always needed to communicate, and this has pushed society to continuously improve their communication systems, from smoke signals to postal services, telegraph to telephone and now the development of 5G infrastructures around the globe.

Radical innovation occurs completely at random; it's not planned and its outcome is unforeseeable. Most of the greatest breakthroughs were triggered not by necessity but by accident. This was the case with the discovery of penicillin. Alexander Fleming, a British researcher often described as a rather messy scientist, came back to his lab from a two weeks' vacation one day in 1928 and found a green mold growing on the dishes of staphylococci bacteria he'd left out. Examining the mold, he noticed that it was killing off the staphylococci. So he isolated the mold, grew more of it, and then experimented to see how much other bacteria it could kill. Quite a lot, it turned out. Penicillin has since become the most widely used antibiotic in the world, has saved countless lives and its discovery earned Fleming a Nobel Prize.

People usually associate innovators with inventors. However, as we can see, that's not entirely accurate. Innovators are more so problem solvers and entrepreneurs. They use their intuition to create new markets or to find a market application for what has already been invented. They improve or adapt it to the consumer demographic they seek or to the industry in which they operate. And it's amazing how much technology sits inside closets, unused, just waiting to be applied.

Steve Jobs is a perfect example of a true innovator. After visiting the Xerox labs and seeing the first computer "mouse," he decided that's exactly what he wanted for his Apple computers. Except he'd reduce the number of buttons from three to one, cutting the price from $300 to $15, and making it much more accessible. As he said, the key to creativity is to expose yourself to the best things humans have to offer, and then to apply those things to your own work.

Think also about artists: when you ask them where they get their inspiration, they usually list others artists. Painters draw upon the tools, techniques and approaches of other painters; musicians use the instruments and styles of other musicians; writers are influenced by the literature they've read, and so on. Innovators build upon the inventions and innovations of others.

A key aspect of innovation, often overlooked, is the execution of the idea rather than the idea in itself. In other words, how we execute a given idea is what really adds value to any innovation.

Although small startups don't have the vast resources necessary to invest heavily in research and development like an established big company, they can still innovate by being more creative and entrepreneurial. So, innovating in a small startup is a bit different than in a big corporation: startuppers have to find ways to get around financial and logistical constraints; generally speaking, they have to test their hypotheses directly in the market, collecting feedback from users. This feedback is essential in understanding the behavior of users, and far more effective than just listening to what users say.

Here are four practical ways a small startups can harness innovation:

Entrepreneurial Innovation ➔ As we said, innovators are not quite inventors, but rather entrepreneurs. So much unutilized technology sits on dusty shelves waiting for a market application. An example of this is aeroponic technology, which was developed by NASA for growing plants vertically, without soil, so astronauts could grow fresh vegetables in space. A small startup named neoFarms harnessed this technology for people living in an urban environment, allowing them to grow small, stackable, fresh gardens in their small apartments. In the same way, Elon Musk utilized reusable rocket technologies invented decades ago by the Soviet Union for his SpaceX program.

Problem-Solving Innovation ➔ For the most part, new innovations stem from a problem in the market, or a market inefficiency. So, it's important to identify these problems and inefficiencies and test your solutions in the market. At the beginning of their journey, the founders of Airbnb realized that when a big event such as a concert, fair or exhibition came to town, it was hard for visitors to find available hotel rooms. Their company gave local residents the opportunity to fill this gap in the market, and rent out their unutilized spaces. Find inefficiencies and validate your solutions.

Failed Innovation ➔ It's essential to learn from the failures of others; you can study hundreds of failures at www.autopsy.io or Failory.com. Once you understand why they failed, you can build from the ashes, improving or adding a twist. In countless cases, the first attempt at something failed and paved the way for the second attempt, which crossed the finish line. This is the case with Google, which overtook Yahoo, or how Facebook improved on MySpace, or even when the battle for the telephone was won by Alexander Graham Bell over Antonio Meucci.

The Telephone Battle—Case Study

In the 1830s, the inventor Antonio Meucci, while attempting to treat illnesses with electric shocks, found that sound could travel by electrical impulses through a copper wire. Sensing something groundbreaking in this discovery, he moved to Staten Island to develop the first telephone prototype. When his wife became paralyzed in 1860, he held a public demonstration of its uses, rigging a system to link her bedroom with his workshop.

But, despite the potential of the "talking telegraph," Meucci struggled to master English and failed to find financial backing. His wife sold his prototypes for $6 to a secondhand shop, and although his models became more sophisticated, eventually including an inductor around a cylindric iron core that would be used for decades, Meucci couldn't afford the $250 needed for a definitive patent. So, in 1871, he filed a one-year renewable notice for an impending patent. Three years later, he couldn't afford the $10 to renew it. He sent a prototype and technical details to the Western Union telegraph company, but failed to win a meeting with its executives. When he asked for his materials to be returned, he was told they had been lost. Two years later, Alexander Graham Bell, who shared a laboratory with Meucci, filed a patent for a telephone, made a lucrative deal with Western Union and became a celebrity.

Although he wasn't the first to experiment with telephonic devices, Bell was the first to develop a commercially viable telephone on the foundation of Meucci's innovations, around which a successful business could be built. Bell adopted carbon transmitters similar to Edison's transmitters and adapted telephone exchanges and switching plug boards developed for telegraphy. Thomas A. Watson and other Bell engineers invented numerous other improvements in telephony.

To summarize Bell's achievements, he was an astute businessman with influential and wealthy friends who succeeded where Meucci failed.

Pivotal innovation➜ Many of the world's greatest innovations happened randomly—think about how Viagra was discovered. Startup founders must always be ready to quickly switch business models according to the needs of the market, like the CEO of Pedego Electric Bikes. The process of developing a pivotal innovation requires relentless testing, and to constantly learn from mistakes. The more mistakes we make, the more we learn.

A Pivoting Business Model—Case Study

Don DiCostanzo, a seasoned entrepreneur, decided to establish an electric bike company, Pedego Bikes. His target customers were elderly people who still enjoyed staying active but needed the support of an electric motor. Finding a Chinese factory to manufacture the bikes was a predictable struggle. However, an even bigger roadblock was distribution in the United States, as bike stores shunned the product. "It was a narrow funnel to start with and they just would not let us in," he said. "They think electric bikes are cheating." Online prospects were just as poor because people want to try bikes before buying them.

For a while, DiCostanzo worked with friends who, in turn, sold the bikes to their own friends at hosted parties—hardly a sustainable business model. Unwilling to go into retail, the company was out of ideas. Then, one day in 2011, a customer asked if he could open his own branded Pedego store. DiCostanzo realized that his business was not about selling e-bikes to consumers, but about giving everyone the opportunity to open an e-bike store in their community. This gave birth to his business model—DiCostanzo opened a franchise of e-bikes, and it receives roughly four hundred inquiries a year.

The Liquid Phase

Every innovation starts with a liquid phase, when it's not yet clear what it's best used for, or what its best design is.

Artificial Intelligence (AI) is a perfect example of this. AI is currently experiencing an extreme liquid phase.

There are so many different types and frameworks of AI that are currently being experimented with, such as:

- Reactive AI
- Limited Memory
- Theory of Mind
- Self-Awareness
- Artificial Narrow Intelligence
- Artificial General Intelligence
- Artificial Super Intelligence

Though, no one has yet cracked the nut of AI and established a dominant design. This is because we've not yet unanimously agreed upon on what *intelligence* truly is. The same phenomenon occurred in the early days of aviation, when we didn't yet fully understand the laws of aerodynamics, and we experienced a proliferation of many fascinating and somewhat odd flying machines around the world. The airplane design, as we know it today, became dominant only when aerodynamic laws were fully understood.

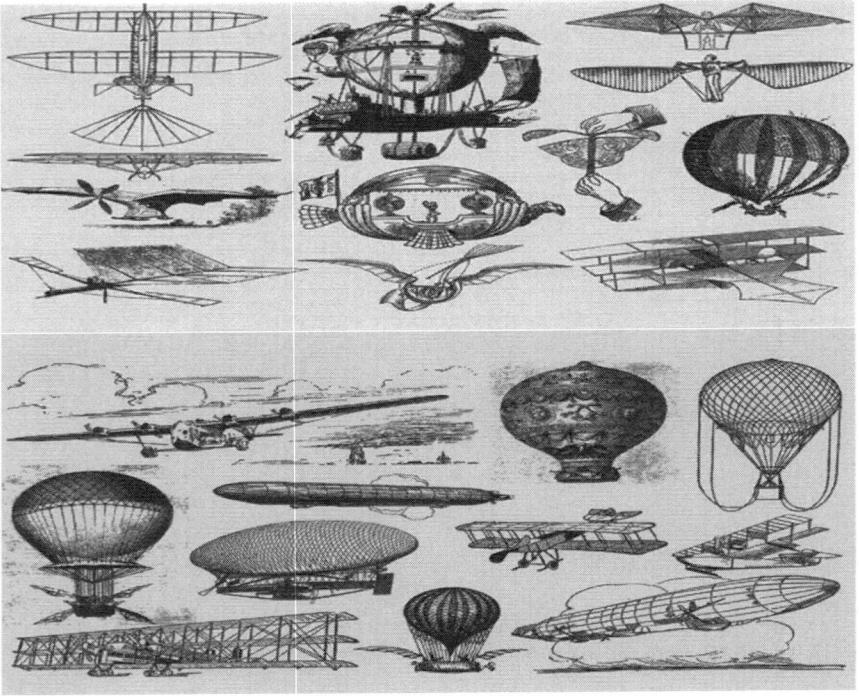

The Five Triggers of Innovation

Innovation is triggered when the following factors take place in any organization:

1. Communication: If people cannot communicate the how, why and what of innovation to each other, the chances of progress are low. Looking back at history, we can clearly see how societies developed faster when interactions intensified. It's not a coincidence that progress stagnated in Europe during the Middle Ages when entire communities were locked up in castles and feudal estate.

   Similarly, the Chinese built the Great Wall in order to protect their advanced and civilized culture from so-called "barbarians," and ended up cutting themselves off from the outside world. After many centuries of relative isolation, the Chinese then realized they'd fallen behind so many of these "barbarians."

   Innovative companies need to avoid at all cost silos and barriers in their organization.

2. Competition: During the Cold War, a proliferation of new innovations stemmed from the heavy competition between the United States and the

Soviet Union. This could be seen in the arms and the space race, but also in other facets of society such as sports, science, computers and health. Startups should encourage competition within their team.

3. Cross-pollination: Being able to connect, combine and reorganize different principles from different disciplines and industries is essential to innovation, and a key part of the creative process. Along with the ability to reframe problems, it engages the human imagination, the innovation engine. For instance, realizing that agricultural machines can be adapted into auto vehicles to transport individuals. Or how microwaves produced by radar systems during World War II can be used as a kitchen appliance to cook popcorns.

   The use of cross-functional teams is strongly encouraged. Also, teams with diverse skill sets and background are ideal.

4. Freedom: Freedom to a broader extent is a key trigger to innovation. When individual lacks freedom in any sort of oppressive structure, they lose the ability to be creative and then innovate.

   Flat organization and open-door policy are always preferred over multi-layered hierarchical structures.

5. Necessity: Necessities, like survival during extreme events such as wars, natural disasters or epidemics, always spur innovation. Global warming is causing entire industries to reinvent themselves and create sustainable, renewable energy technology and products like electric vehicles. Epidemic breakouts like the Ebola outbreak in 2014 accelerated R&D efforts in finding cures and vaccines.
   Instilling a sense of urgency, having a clear mission and sharing a common goal are the key for every innovative startup.

The Ideal Innovation Hub: The Renaissance Case Study

The Renaissance so perfectly demonstrates all of the triggers previously discussed. During the roughly 200 years, the Italian city-states, packed with all their many geniuses, were producing innovations at an unprecedented rate. It was a rebirth and rediscovery of mathematics, philosophy, astrology, astronomy, science, literature and art. The Renaissance represents the ideal innovation hothouse by integrating all of the five triggers.

1. Communication: With the advent of the printing press, knowledge was for the first time accessible to people outside of the clergy and the aristocracy. Meanwhile, the discoveries of new sea routes to Asia and of the American continents opened up interactions between merchants, traders and entire populaces previously isolated from one another.

2. Competition: Rivalries between the Italian city-states and their leaders were fierce. The two stars of the age, Leonardo Da Vinci and Michelangelo, couldn't stomach one another, and that contributed to all their fine work. The decades-long feud between Lorenzo Ghiberti and Filippo Brunelleschi, meanwhile, had the same effect. When Brunelleschi lost the commission to build the Gates of Paradise in Florence to Ghiberti, he traveled to Rome to learn new skills and began to study ancient structures like the Pantheon. He then brought these lessons home, and eventually built Florence's iconic landmark, the Duomo.

3. Cross-pollination: The revival of mathematics and the use of proportions led to breakthroughs in art and architecture, especially with the introduction of linear perspective and the vanishing point. The mastermind behind these principles was the author of three mathematical treatises and a wonderful artist, Piero della Francesca, whose perspective paintings and impressive figures showed unprecedented technique. Modern architecture and design principles still follow in his footsteps.

4. Freedom: There was a major shift in human belief from religion to humanism during the Renaissance. Intellectuals, artisans and even commoners concluded that the church was never a responsible source of their behavior and beliefs toward God and fellow men and they themselves are responsible for the actions.

5. Necessity: Cities like Florence remind us that war and catastrophe can yield surprising benefits. Florence blossomed only a few decades after the Black Death decimated Europe, and in part because of it. Horrible as it was, the plague shook up the rigid social order, leading directly to urbanization and intellectual revolution.

Innovative Technology in Machiavelli's Strategies

Machiavelli understood that early gunpowder weapons weren't so effective in combat. People have misinterpreted this, thinking that he meant we shouldn't rely on technological innovations. However, the real takeaway here is simply to use the most reliable technology available. In most cases, reliable technology will win over innovative technology.

Numerous companies, especially small ones, have failed because they bet on the wrong horse, simply because it was the novelty on the scene. Many people tend to forget that every new technology comes with the hidden cost of trying something for the first time. Regardless of tests and simulations, outcomes remain unpredictable—it takes many years before the newest technology becomes reliable.

Machiavelli knew this very well, which is why he discouraged the use of gunpowder; in his days, a crossbow and a sword were much more effective.

Indeed, it was only until the end of World War I that rifles finally dropped bayonets and became a reliable standalone technology. For centuries, guns needed bayonets because they were so inaccurate, didn't hold enough rounds, were slow to recharge and jammed frequently.

As stated by the famous Russian general Alexander Suvorov in 1796, "The bullet is a mad thing; only the bayonet knows what it is about."

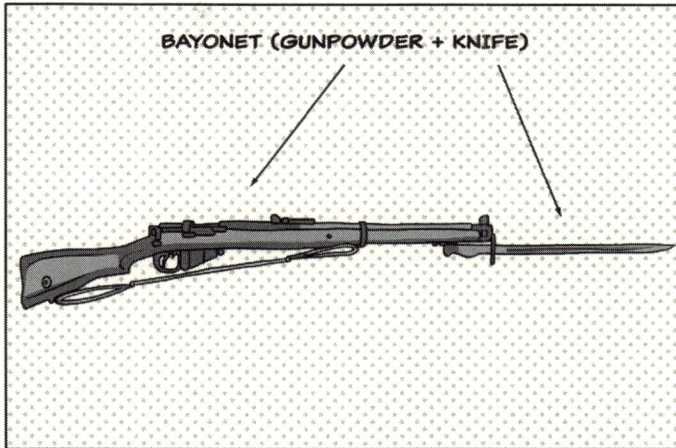

BAYONET (GUNPOWDER + KNIFE)

So, if something is new, fancy or techie, it doesn't mean it will be more effective. In a startup, it's all about getting the job done in the easiest and fastest way; given their small size and limited resources, startups have a much better chance of winning over bigger companies on speed rather than cutting-edge technology. Betting on unreliable technology may indeed prove to be fatal.

During the Vietnam War, the U.S. military may have been hindered by its superior communications and complex technologies—too much information had to be to be processed, which made for slower response times. The Viet Cong, on the other hand, depended on a simple network of informers, not gadgetry—they made quicker decisions and were nimbler on the ground as a result of it.

As Elon Musk admitted, excessive automation at Tesla—putting too many robots in Tesla's lone auto-factory—was a mistake. He thought that robots would give his company a crazy competitive advantage over his competitors, but he underestimated human flexibility. He cites the excessive use of robots as a major factor holding Tesla back from making more Model 3s. The whole complex network of conveyor belts he had established was eventually axed.

Automation "is expensive and is statistically inversely correlated to quality," Musk notes. One tenet of lean production is "stabilize the process, and only then automate." If you automate first, you get automated errors.

Case Study: Toyota—The Adoption Process of New Technology

At Toyota, new technology is introduced only after direct experimentation conducted by a broad cross-section of people. Great lengths are gone to analyze the impact it may have on the existing process.

First, the value of that particular technology is evaluated. New opportunities to eliminate waste and improve the workflow are sought. Toyota will then use a pilot area to improve the technology with existing equipment.

Only after being thoroughly acid tested and all potential conflicts are resolved is the new technology accepted. The guiding principle is then to design and use it to support the workflow and help employees perform better within Toyota's high standards. This means the technology has to be highly visual and intuitive. Ideally, it will be used right there on the work floor rather than in a hidden office so that everyone can continue to evaluate it.

For Toyota, flexibility doesn't mean plugging the latest and greatest technology into operations and struggling to make it fit. They only use reliable, tested technology, adapting it to serve its people and process.

Takeaways

- Innovating is a necessity for startups if they want to find space in the market. Startups have to come out with something new and better.
- Don't waste money on looking for the silver bullet. Innovations happen either incrementally or randomly.
- Before jumping on a new technology, evaluate first if it will add value to your organization. If yes, adapt the technology to your startup rather than adapting your startup to the technology.
- Errors, errors, errors. The more mistakes we make, the faster we learn and the more we can innovate.

Chapter 3

ALLIANCES: KEEPING YOUR FRIENDS CLOSE, AND YOUR ENEMIES EVEN CLOSER

This chapter will illustrate the importance of alliances and agreements, in order to spur the growth of a startup. That is,

- Strategic alliances and acquisitions
- Sucker fish Strategy—how to boost your growth with no effort
- Choosing your allies wisely
- Negotiation one-on-one

HEY LORENZO!

I DIDN'T KNOW YOU RAN THIS EARLY IN THE MORNING.

SO, AS I'M SURE YOU KNOW, LORENZO, THERE'S BEEN A LOT OF BUZZ ABOUT YOUR STARTUP LATELY.

IT'S REALLY AMAZING HOW YOU WERE ABLE TO EMERGE FROM THE SWAMP.

SOME DIDN'T THINK YOU EVER WOULD, BUT NOW YOU'VE CAUGHT THEIR EYE.

I GUESS THAT'S GOOD NEWS.

SLAM!
YAP
YAP
YAP
YAP
HUFF
PUFF
YAP
YAP
YAP
YAP
GASP!
GASP!
GASP!
I DON'T KNOW. SOMETHING SMELLS FISHY TO ME...
BECAUSE WE'RE DEALING WITH AUT CAESAR?

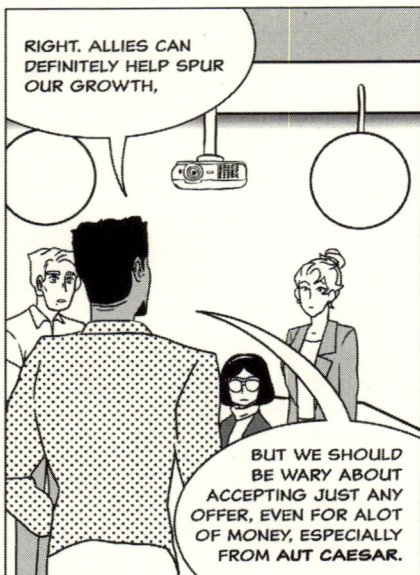

RIGHT. ALLIES CAN DEFINITELY HELP SPUR OUR GROWTH,

BUT WE SHOULD BE WARY ABOUT ACCEPTING JUST ANY OFFER, EVEN FOR ALOT OF MONEY, ESPECIALLY FROM **AUT CAESAR.**

YOU'RE RIGHT. MACHIAVELLI ALSO SAYS THAT ALLIES HAVE THE POWER TO WIN YOUR WAR OR RUIN YOU.

WHAT OTHER OPTIONS DO WE HAVE?

WELL, UNLESS WE CAN FIND OTHER STARTUPS THAT ARE AT THE SAME LEVEL AS US, ANY TYPE OF ALLIANCE MIGHT PROVE DANGEROUS.

SO HOW WILL WE KEEP GROWING?

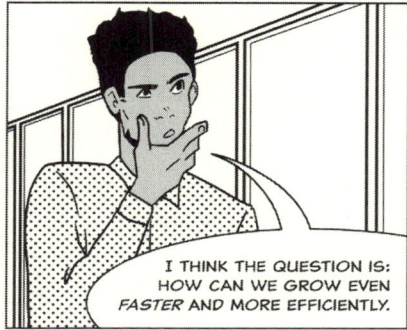

I THINK THE QUESTION IS: HOW CAN WE GROW EVEN *FASTER* AND MORE EFFICIENTLY.

THERE'S ANOTHER STRATEGY WE CAN USE...

WITHOUT SELLING OUR SOULS?

YES, WE'LL USE THE SUCKERFISH STRATEGY — IT'S PROVED SUCCESSFUL FOR MANY STARTUPS, HELPING THEM GROW INTO BIG COMPANIES.

STARTUPS CAN USE THE SAME CONCEPT TO BE EFFECTIVE AT ALMOST ZERO COST. LET'S TAKE A LOOK AT HOW THIS HAS BEEN DONE IN THE PAST...

BIG FISH	INEFFICIENCIES	SUCKER FISH
CRAIGSLIST	1. LOW QUALITY PHOTOS 2. OBSOLETE UX – UI 3. HARD TO FIND HOTEL ROOMS DURING LOCAL EVENTS	AIRBNB
TAXI & BLACK CAR COMPANIES	1. SUPPLY & DEMAND MISMATCH 2. LACK OF TRANSPARENCY ON RIDE FARES 3. JUNKIE CARS	UBER
EBAY	1. PAYMENT INEFFICIENCY 2. FRAUDS 3. TRANSPARENCY	PAYPAL
CRAFT FAIRS	1. HARD TO SCALE FOR CITY CRAFT FAIRS 2. LACK OF GLOBAL EXPOSURE FOR ARTISAN / ARTIST	ETSY
COLLEGE CAMPUSES	1. HARD TO KEEP IN TOUCH WITH FRIENDS AFTER COLLEGE 2. STUDENTS' NEED FOR VISIBILITY (BIG EGO / NARCISSISTIC NEED)	FB

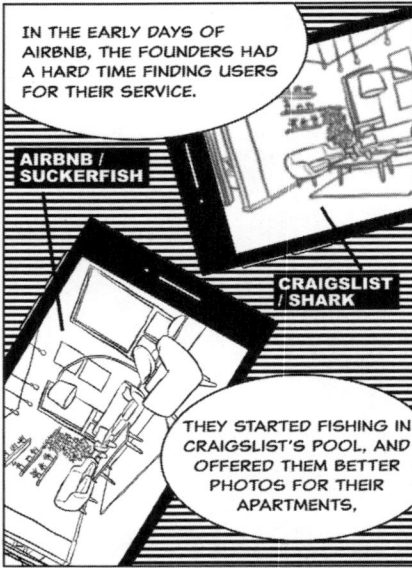

EVEN PAYPAL WISELY USED THE SUCKERFISH STRATEGY BY INTEGRATING ITS SAFE PAYMENT SOLUTION TO EBAY'S PLATFORM.

BROKEN LASER POINTER $14.83

WITH THE SAFETY PAYPAL PROVIDED FOR TRANSACTIONS, NOT ONLY DID EBAY BENEFIT,

BUT PAYPAL BEGAN ATTRACTING MORE USERS, GROWING AT THE SPEED OF LIGHT.

HOW ABOUT HOW FACEBOOK STARTED GROWING ITS SOCIAL NETWORK BY LEVERAGING THE PLATFORM OF COLLEGE CAMPUSES?

INDEED.

STUDENTS DIDN'T KNOW HOW TO STAY IN CONTACT WITH THEIR FRIENDS AFTER COLLEGE, AND ALSO ALWAYS NEED TO FEED THEIR EGOS WITH RECOGNITION.

THAT'S WHY COLLEGE CAMPUSES AND STUDENTS ACTED AS THE PERFECT LAUNCHING PAD FOR FACEBOOK.

Chapter 3: Alliances

According to Machiavelli, staying neutral is a bad idea. So, whether you're a young startup or an established one, it's important to form **alliance**s. The benefits of doing so are vast and include sharing resources, lowering costs, faster growth and knowledge transfer.

So let's take a look at *how* this can be done, keeping in mind that most startups don't have the money to acquire another company. And there's always the risk of being acquired by bigger companies.

Choosing Your Allies

When targeting a potential ally, ask yourself: what will they provide? Do they have something unique? If not, where else can you find it?

Be wary of allying yourself with someone much bigger and stronger than you are. Many founders look for an early exit, thinking this to be the best possible thing that could happen to them. But this usually leads to their companies disappearing, as most benefits go to the acquiring company.

Indeed, although some big companies just want to acquire the technology of a smaller, more innovative one, they mostly just want to get rid of a potential future threat (such as LinkedIn and Refresh.io, or Facebook and Instagram).

Small startups should therefore keep battling in the arena and try to establish themselves in a local area or in a specific market segment. Or by offering a high level of innovation, which bigger companies don't have. This will help attract the interest of bigger companies and useful allies alike. And it can eventually lead to a big offer—by rejecting it, you'll only draw more attention.

Consider Snapchat versus Facebook. It's not often that a small startup refuses a billions of dollars offer, as Snapchat did after they **segmented** Facebook to create a fun and more innovative app specifically designed for younger Facebook users.

Facebook saw that the number of its teenaged users was decreasing, and felt that Snapchat would eventually make it obsolete. So, they tried to adopt the same strategy that had worked so well when acquiring Instagram and WhatsApp, and in 2013, Mark Zuckerberg offered Snapchat $3 billion. However, Snapchat responded, "No thank you!"

By turning Facebook down, Snapchat's value—and the number of its users—increased dramatically. In 2016, the company went public and the founders' stake was worth more than what Facebook had offered for the entire company. (The app added 8 million new users daily in the first three months of 2017, demonstrating a year-on-year growth of 36 percent. With a projected value of $17 a share, cofounder Evan Spiegel will now be worth around $4.49 billion, and cofounder Bobby Murphy will be worth around $3.86 billion.)

Not happy with the failed acquisition, Facebook began adopting an aggressive matching strategy to counteract Snapchat, blatantly cloning their core features. The result is that Facebook's family of standalone apps—Instagram, Messenger and even WhatsApp—look a lot like Snapchat. Zuckerberg now believes the future of communication on Facebook will be through the phone's camera—a concept Snapchat pioneered.

Another thing to keep in mind: bad allies can drag you down, which happened to Yahoo:

In the late 1990s, Yahoo was king of the internet, the most visited site by 40 times over the second-most-visited site. To consolidate its position, Yahoo started an acquisition binge on many different companies, including Broadcast.com founded by Christopher Jaeb, which was later led by Todd Wagner and Mark Cuban.

Yahoo paid $5.7 billion (almost 350 times Broadcast.com's value) for a company with little revenue and almost no profit. However, due to the slow internet connection of the time, Yahoo soon had to shut down the service.

Moral of the story: Mark Cuban became a billionaire, bought the Dallas Mavericks and sits as an investor on the TV show "Shark Tank," while Yahoo never regained its prominent place.

The Suckerfish Strategy

Because it's not always easy to attract useful allies and share the resource of bigger companies, small startups should consider using the Suckerfish Strategy. Suckerfish are those little fish that cling to the belly of big sharks, swim with minimal effort and steal the sharks' prey.

Let's take a look at how this strategy can be applied harnessing already existing infrastructures.

Airbnb

In the early days of Airbnb, cofounders Brian Chesky and Joe Gebbia had a hard time finding users for their service. Especially because they had to first find people willing to list their homes. And how many people want to let a stranger stay in their place? It's not like the founders could go around knocking on doors.

So they thought like customers themselves and realized they'd visit Craigslist if they ever needed to find a place to stay. Confident they could do a much better job listing apartments than the online classified site, they decided to first siphon away Craigslist users. To do that, they created software to hack and extract the contact info of property owners with listings on Craigslist. They then pitched them to list on Airbnb as well.

The strategy worked. With nothing to lose, the property owners doubled their chances of finding a potential renter, and Airbnb had a ready supply of listings with which it could attract further users.

Uber

Ride-sharing app Uber pursued a similar strategy. Rather than starting out with Uber Pool or Uber X, where drivers use their own cars, they started using private black car companies driven by professional drivers. That way, they could ensure users had a great experience virtually every time. They could then rely on users to spread the news of that experience.

Since Uber's main competitors were yellow cab companies, they researched which cities had the biggest discrepancy between the supply and demand for taxis. They then launched during times when that demand was likely to be the highest. For example, during the holidays. It also ran promotions during large concerts or sporting events, when big crowds all needed cabs at the same time, and people would be more likely to take a chance with an unfamiliar company.

In this way, Uber quickly acquired a large group of users, knowing that it was only a matter of time before people started using their service to go to work, shop, etc. The service was simply—and remains—too convenient to resist, and they built it on the back of what was already in place.

Etsy

At its inception, Etsy—which serves as an online marketplace for craft vendors—started its business with an offline strategy: its founders scoured craft fairs across the country to identify the best vendors at each. They then pitched these venders to open up an online store on the site. Soon, their customers were all shopping online, so others artisans followed the customers.

Other examples:

PayPal: integrated its service to facilitate payments within eBay's platform.
Facebook: used the college campus as a launch pad.

Again: all these integrations worked so well because they were fixing market inefficiencies:

Airbnb ➜ Craigslist

People needing places to stay had to deal with low-quality pictures, hard-to-find hotel rooms, high rates during events, etc.

Uber ➜ Taxi Companies

Matching supply with demand, solving lack of transparency on rates, bad drivers, etc.

Etsy ➜ Craft Fairs

Making shopping more convenient, giving artisan/artists global exposure, etc.

PayPal ➜ eBay

Users were suffering over payment safety, transparency issues, fraud, etc.

Facebook ➜ College Campus

Students wanted a way to keep in touch with friends even after college, and to show off publicly and to their friends
Bear in mind: A well-executed Suckerfish Strategy is not simply about poaching into competitor's users. It's about providing something better than what users had before.

Negotiation One-on-One

Knowing the basics of negotiating, whether for the lease of your first office or to seal an exit deal, is paramount for small startups. Because of course, small startups don't have much leverage.

Following Machiavelli's principles where whenever possible it is always better to be loved than feared. The elements of a successful negotiation include fairness, mutual benefit and maintaining a relationship. These aren't always easy to find, however, as negotiations are unpredictable, and psychological factors (such as ego, insecurities, pride, power, mood, etc.) always play an important role. To minimize uncertainties and get the best possible outcome, startup founders should have a few things clearly in mind before walking into the negotiating room:

- **Define your BATNA** (Best Alternative to a Negotiated Agreement). Your BATNA, a combination of price, terms and deliverables, is the most advantageous course of action you can take if negotiations fall through, and is the driving force behind every successful negotiator. Without a clear BATNA, you'll have no negotiation roadmap and won't be prepared to deal with the possible consequences of a no deal. Remember never accept something less than your BATNA.

- **Have More Than One Option**. Increasing the number of alternatives in a negotiation is just as important as knowing your BATNA. One of the reasons why the strategies of the great conqueror Napoleon were so successful is that he was able to come up with far more alternatives during battles than his opponents. The more alternatives you have to work with, the more options you have to offer, and the greater your chances of closing a good deal. And even if you don't have many alternatives, act as if you do. It's ok to bluff in that case!

- **Address the Elephant in the Room Last**. When you have a lot of points to negotiate, start off with easiest, even if seems logical to begin with the deal killers. There are two reasons for this. First, resolving easy issues creates momentum and may lead to inventive solutions. You may even get your counterpart to see the value of exploring new approaches. Second, if you concede something early on, your counterpart will be more willing to concede something more important to you down the road. Just like in chess, sometimes you have to sacrifice a bishop to get the queen.

- **Overcoming Road Blocks**. Not every negotiation will go smoothly. When parties have locked into their positions, it's difficult to win arguments, however brilliant they may be. It may seems counterintuitive, but under those circumstances, persuasion is more a function of listening and understanding. When you listen without defending, you diffuse tensions without making any concessions. This doesn't mean to nod your head and say "uh-huh," but to maintain eye contact and a neutral expression. This will also help you better understand if your counterpart is digging in their heels for objective constraints or subjective reasons, such as ego/power issues. You'll know if they're just trying to take advantage of you.

Try to be always objective; if you can't meet your counterpart's request, it should only be because of objective constraints outside of your control. For example "I'd like to meet you expectations however I can't pay the asking price because the bank didn't extend my credit line."

If conceding a point to your counterpart will not harm your startup, you should do it. However, keep in mind that every concession is likely to have a different value for the buyer and seller, so begin by giving small things that your counterparts value highly, but which have little incremental cost for your startup. For example:
- Payment options
- Quantity discounts

- Bundling with other purchases
- Promotions
- Complimentary service
- Timing of delivery
- Credit
- Customization
- Assurance of quality
- Preferred treatment

   Ultimately, in case it's not possible to find an agreement, withdraw from the negotiation by asking to reschedule the meeting another day or to consult your cofounders/advisors in order to suggest a more constructive agenda.

- **Don't Just Shake Hands**. Negotiations can get confusing, and often what's said can get distorted or misinterpreted. So, always summarize what's been already been accomplished and sketch out what still needs to be done. Brief but frequent recaps actually maintain momentum and keeps everyone on the same page. Putting everything in writing ensures everyone is held accountable for their statements.

- **Every Offer Is Too Low**. Whether you are making the offer or receiving it, every offer will always be too low. So if someone is making you an offer, be ready to counter it by increasing it. When you make an offer, start low as they probably will do the same no matter how high your figure is. So be ready to counter every offer.

Also never round your offer numbers (e.g., $1,000, $15,000, $800). Leave some decimals in it (e.g., $1,275, $16,325, $879.82). That will decrease the range of their counteroffer as your counterpart will be more likely start to negotiate from the decimals. In addition, it will show you have done your due diligence in coming out with the exact figure.

- **Trade Space for Time**. Time is a key factor in negotiations. Although we've all learned that time is money, when it comes to negotiations, it's quite the opposite: *not* taking time is money.

   In negotiations, whoever can wait longer has a position of power. Don't let your counterpart rush you into making an unfavorable or rash agreement. Instead, determine first who's holding the resources in the negotiation; that will help you understand the roles and how best to act. If you are the party that is controlling the resources, don't fall into the trap of closing a deal too soon, as your counterpart will be trying to prevent you from looking around for alternatives. They'll be trying to make you to commit by instilling in you the fear of missing out by showing you scarcity, exclusivity or fierce competition.

Throw in some counteroffers and concede something small to gain time. Once you're deep in negotiations, it will be then easier to leverage on what you want, because your counterpart will feel like they've wasted a lot of time if there's no deal. Indeed, they'll likely settle for something less, rather than walk away with nothing and start all over again with a stranger.

Case study: Napoleon's Campaign in Russia

Napoleon's Grande Armee was far superior to the Russian army. The Russian general Kutuzov was well aware of this, and knew that he'd always lose a head-to-head battle. His strategy, therefore, was to retreat deep into the heart of Siberia in summer, and let the Grande Armee chase him, leaving behind just burnt villages and fields so it couldn't live off the land. He'd only engage the enemy to tempt them on and give Napoleon the illusion of winning the war—he was essentially trading space for time, allowing Napoleon to come forward waiting for winter to come.

Finally, it did, and the Grande Armee found itself exhausted, demoralized and surrounded by ice with no supplies hundreds of miles away from home. The enemy, meanwhile, was still at large. Desperately, Napoleon ordered the retreat, but it was too late. Kutuzov started to counterattack the retreating forces in a devastating display of guerrilla warfare and the Grande Armee, the largest army ever assembled at that time, was massacred. By the end of the campaign, 500,000 of the 685,000 soldiers did not make it back home.

Chapter 4

LEADERSHIP: BECOMING THE PRINCE

This chapter delves into what it means to be a good leader in terms of traits, psychology and social interactions, teaching to startuppers how they can become the virtuous leader of the ideal, successful company by considering the following:

- Build a strong team: How to recruit the right people
- How to structure your company
- Mentorship
- Psychology of startups
- The Machiavellian leader in a startup
- Creating a legend: Making yourself larger than life

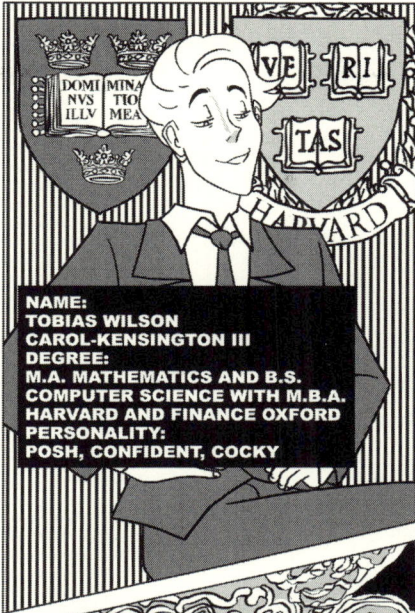

NAME:
TOBIAS WILSON
CAROL-KENSINGTON III
DEGREE:
M.A. MATHEMATICS AND B.S.
COMPUTER SCIENCE WITH M.B.A.
HARVARD AND FINANCE OXFORD
PERSONALITY:
POSH, CONFIDENT, COCKY

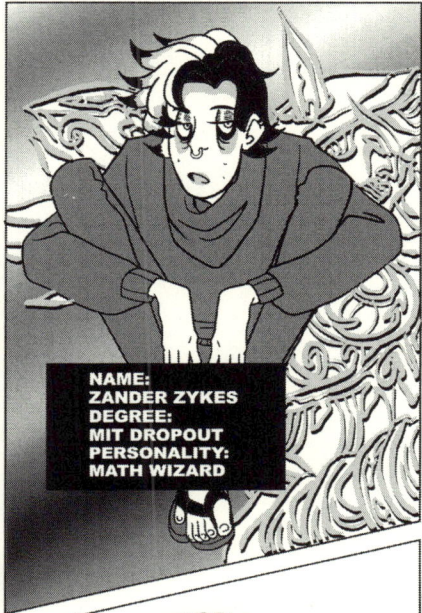

NAME:
ZANDER ZYKES
DEGREE:
MIT DROPOUT
PERSONALITY:
MATH WIZARD

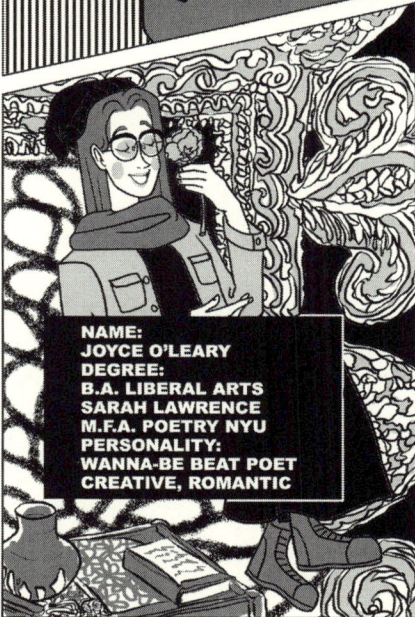

NAME:
JOYCE O'LEARY
DEGREE:
B.A. LIBERAL ARTS
SARAH LAWRENCE
M.F.A. POETRY NYU
PERSONALITY:
WANNA-BE BEAT POET
CREATIVE, ROMANTIC

NAME:
ROBERTO VALTURIO
DEGREE:
B.S. COMPUTER SCIENCE
CUNY STATE
PERSONALITY:
EAGER, ENTHUSIASTIC,
CURIOUS, CRAFTY, CORKY

NAME:
ELON MUSK
STYLE:
THE DISRUPTIVE INNOVATOR
MOTTO:
"FAILURE IS NOT AN OPTION HERE. IF THINGS ARE NOT FAILING, YOU'RE NOT INNOVATING ENOUGH."
NAME:
RICHARD BRANSON
NAME:
THE SOCIAL CAPITALIST
MOTTO:
"THE WAY YOU TREAT YOUR EMPLOYEES IS THE WAY THEY WILL TREAT YOUR CUSTOMERS."
NAME:
STEVE JOBS
STYLE:
THE AMBITIOUS GENIUS
MOTTO:
"I WANT TO PUT A DING IN THE UNIVERSE."
NAME:
JACK MA
STYLE:
THE REGULAR GUY WHO FAILED 100 TIMES
MOTTO:
"WHEN KFC CAME TO CHINA, 24 PEOPLE WENT FOR THE JOB, 23 PEOPLE WERE ACCEPTED. I WAS THE ONLY GUY LEFT OUT."
YES, I KNOW HOW IMPORTANT IT IS TO STUDY THE PAST AND LEARN FROM IT
A PRINCE SHOULD... EXERCISE HIS MIND BY READING THE HISTORIES OF GREAT MEN AND HOW THEY WAGED WAR,
IN ORDER TO IMITATE THEM
GREAT LEADERS HAVE ALWAYS TRIED TO EMULATE THE QUALITIES OF THOSE WORTHY EXAMPLES WHO PRECEDED THEM
BY STUDYING THEIR PRECEPTS IN GOOD TIMES, THE PRINCE WILL BE READY WHEN FORTUNE CHANGES

"A prince should have no other aim or thought, nor take up any other thing for his study but war and its organization and discipline, for that is the only art that is necessary to one who commands. Even in peacetime, a prince must concentrate on war by exercises and by study."

Chapter 4: Leadership

Building a Strong Team

The most valuable asset of a startup is its team. Every Venture Capital out there is more likely to invest in a startup with a B product and an A team rather than vice versa.

This suggests to every startup founder that building a strong team is key to success of your company.

You can build a strong team in two ways:

• By recruiting talent from other companies
• By training your team in-house to build core competencies

The risk with recruiting talents from other companies is hiring mercenaries. By training your team, it may take a little longer but in the long run it will pay off as it creates a sustainable advantage to your startup.

Of course, building a strong team can be one of the most challenging things for a founder in a startup's early stages. Attracting top talents with the most developed skill set is especially difficult.

But talent and skill aren't everything—it's even more important to consider potential team members based on their personalities and attitudes.

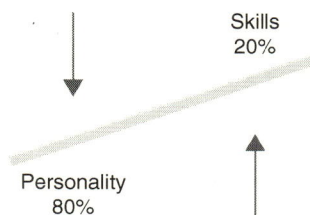

Skills
20%

Personality
80%

In the Information Age, skills can be learned somewhat easily. A good personality, however, can't. And without a good personality, skills are useless, and in some cases, even detrimental.

So, try to find people with not necessarily the best qualities but the *right* qualities, and keep investing in their training.

Speaking of the *right* qualities, look for the following personality traits:

• Enthusiastic
• Loyal
• Risk takers
• Drive

- Curiosity
- Determination
- Stamina

Keep in mind that all team members must be ready to be work full-time. In a startup, there's no such thing as a part-time job, as it takes so much energy to lift it from the ground. Remote positions also simply don't work in the long run.

Everyone must have the same interest and the same involvement. This will prevent motivational misalignment. The team must be homogenous in terms of personality types, but with very different skills to complement one another.

Remember: Same Motivation, Different Skills.

Recruiting

When recruiting soldiers for your army, as noted above, **enthusiasm** is essential. In the early stages of your startup, you might find it quite easy to find talents willing to work with you for free simply because they're motivated by their enthusiasm for the project. Just keep in mind that these people are your most precious assets—don't ever take them for granted.

Enthusiasm, meanwhile, has its limits with all the inevitable ups and downs of a startup. So, to keep them motivated, use financial rewards and couple these with training sessions.

Your **reputation** is fundamental when it comes to attracting the best possible candidates. So, start refining your storytelling to articulate your vision in the most attractive way. More on this below.

In terms of money matters, salaries shouldn't start high. Employees should be rewarded not for what the company is *today* but for what it will be *tomorrow* (i.e., company shares).

Be skeptical of those who join your startup only for money, even if they've got a perfect resume. They won't add much value and during rough seas; they'll always be the first ones to flee. As Machiavelli notes,

> Mercenaries and auxiliaries are dangerous and unreliable. If a mercenary is talented, he will always be trying to increase his power at the prince's expense. If he is incompetent, he will ruin the prince. Only leaders and enterprises that field their own armies can succeed, for mercenaries do nothing but lose. Those who are well armed can live free.

The Psychology of a Startup

Generally, people who are entrepreneurial, energetic, self-starter, motivated and creative—the typical startupper—are more likely to have strong emotional states. Those states may include depression, despair, hopelessness, worthlessness and loss of motivation. And we get it, being a startupper is tough, no one tells you what to do, no roadmaps and there's always a high risk of failure. Three out of four venture-backed startups fail, according to research by Shikhar Ghosh, a Harvard Business School lecturer. In addition, more than 95 percent of startups fall short of their initial projections.

The good news is that the life of a startup is like the mood of a teenager: cyclical. Hopeless bottoms where you might start thinking about bailing and looking for a different ship will soon be met with euphoric highs, where everyone loves being part of the team and is willing to work nights and weekends. So keep the resilience high—no rain, no rainbow. And the rollercoaster ride tends to flatten out with time.

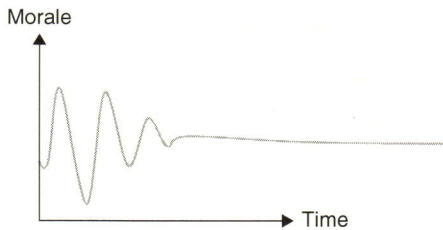

Morale

Time

In order to keep moral high, especially on tough days, founders should surround themselves with people who aren't there simply because they need a job, but because they have a strong belief in what they're building. People who identify strongly with the startup and the founder's vision.

They should also surround themselves with **advisors**.

Every startup should have advisors, consultants or mentors who aren't directly involved with the company, but who are particularly well informed, trusted and experienced. They should be invited regularly (i.e., once a week or once a month, depending on your needs) to discuss where the company is going, to validate ideas (and brainstorm new ones) and to help solve problems from a different angle.

It's good to have more than one advisor—startuppers should always ask a lot of questions to a lot of different people. This is a free way to get ideas. One conversation can be 10 times more insightful than research on Google. However, it's ultimately up to the founders and their team to connect the dots and find the best way to apply all of aggregated advice.

Many startuppers will find that the dots are connected and best ideas come in the most random situations. Such as in the bathroom, before falling asleep at night, while talking to a friend, jogging in Central Park, etc.

This is called **diffuse thinking**.

Unlike **focused thinking**, diffuse thinking happens when you let your mind wander freely, making connections at random. This doesn't happen in any one area of the brain, but all over.

Usually, diffuse thinking happens when you're doing other things. That's why it's important to take breaks, which can actually lead to a major break-through. When your conscious mind is relaxed, your brain can include many more variables, form a creative solution or finally make that link between ideas that's been eluding you.

With focused thinking, your brain processes very specific information deeply; with diffuse thinking, the brain analyzes much more information, but in less depth.

The truth is, when it comes to problem-solving, too much focus can be a bad thing. The longer we keep our brains focused, the more we experience tunnel vision. This blocks our creativity, and our outside-of-the-box thinking.

The **unstoppable mindset** is essential for a startupper—your startup should be your obsession. When we choose to start up, we're not choosing a job or a career but a lifestyle. So it's unacceptable to think that the job ends when you leave the office. It never stops, which can be considered both a blessing and a curse.

For many founders, setting up their office in their garage isn't just a way to reduce costs, but to never disconnect the wires. This isn't to say that you should lock yourself up in a garage without seeing anyone. Quite the opposite: keep open and always seek to use the inputs you receive from the world in a way that benefits your startup. Keep in mind networking will nurture your startup.

A Startup's Structure

Small startups are innovative due to their very structure—they are flat organizations, which allows new and challenging ideas to fly freely, and gives a sense of ownership to everyone. This spurs innovation, because innovation occurs randomly, in **free** and **fun** ecosystems. Communication is not layered or filtered as it is in bigger, hierarchical organizations, where only a small, designated group of people can innovate.

For big organizations like Microsoft, this is a problem. Microsoft started out as a very innovative company; however, as it grew bigger and became increasingly more structured and hierarchical, employees became comfort-able and lost their hunger. The only way to keep innovating for companies like Microsoft is to scout for smaller, more innovative startups filled with fresh, hungry minds and then merge or acquire them.

So, even as you grow, try to find the time to meet with your team and exchange ideas. Here's a good example: Amazon's C-level executives start their day by reading together for 30 minutes in silence, and then comment it freely. Every morning they ask, "How can we innovate?"

Hierarchical versus Flat Organizations

HIERARCHICAL VS. FLAT ORGANIZATIONS

SMALL STARTUPS ARE VERY INNOVATIVE BECAUSE OF THEIR STRUCTURE. USUALLY THEY ARE FLAT ORGANIZATIONS.

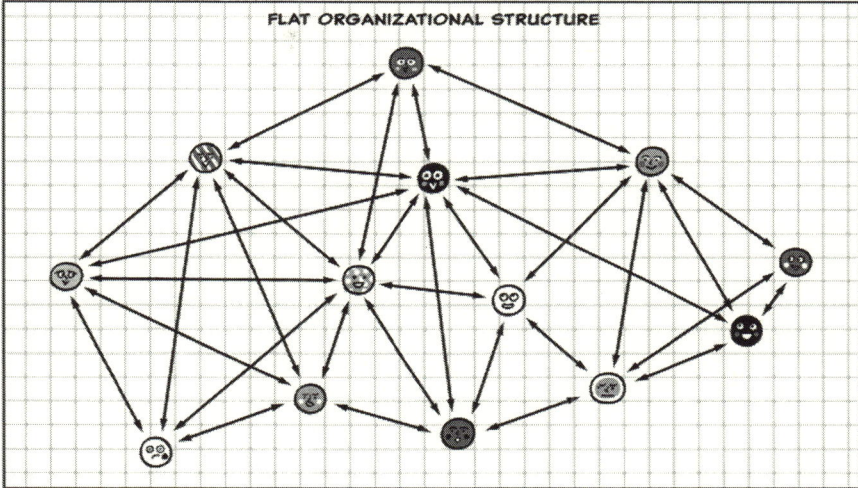

FLAT ORGANIZATIONAL STRUCTURE

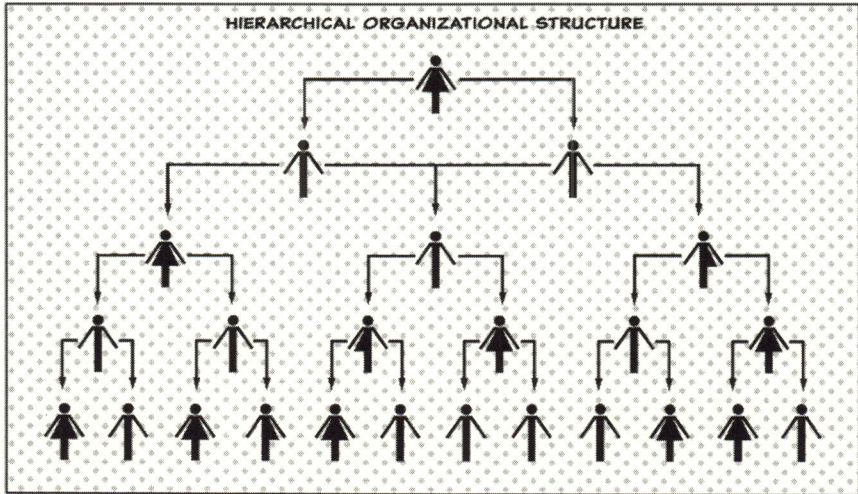

HIERARCHICAL ORGANIZATIONAL STRUCTURE

Being the Prince

> Wherefore, a wise Prince should devise means whereby his subjects may at all times, whether favorable or adverse, feel the need of the State and of him, and they will always be faithful to him.
>
> — Machiavelli, *The Prince*

Discipline is key to sustained growth. Especially in very inherently unstructured organizations like startups. Have a disciplined routine that inspires confidence in your team, which can include having habits or rules followed by everyone in your team (e.g., everyone has to use the same smartphone case or every Wednesday team workout at the gym).

Don't just act in your own interest. If you do, people hardly will be willing to help. You have to think bigger and act in the interest of your team and of everyone your product or service will affect.

Make sure your team knows that *they* have the power to influence the startup's destiny just as much as you do. Be honest with them. Outline and share the hurdles and opportunities that lay ahead, and be ready to take a bullet for them.

- "People will always help you build the world they are a part of."
- Keep your ego in check. Don't let the VC funding get to your head.
- Be ready to make bold and drastic decisions.
  - Be meritocratic
  - See value in people where others don't
  - Choose the road of virtue over shortcuts
  - Empower and give freedom to individuals; welcome ideas that might sound weird at first
  - Reward individual passions
  - Cultivate talents and help them emerge
  - Be obsessed with growth; take every opportunity to expand
  - Invest in team training
  - Listen to your advisors
  - Stay optimistic, especially during tough times
  - Enjoy your work

Creating a Legend: Making Yourself Larger Than Life

> Everyone sees what you appear to be, few experience what you really are. — Machiavelli, *The Prince*

Popularity definitely has its benefits. Doors open without knocking, talented minds want to work with you, e-mails are returned and phone calls are picked up. That's why you see the line between entrepreneurs and celebrities thinning. Entrepreneurs are becoming hybrids of stars and politicians by joining social causes and influencing the masses with their lifestyles, healthy habits and tips for success.

So, don't hesitate to get involved. Be vocal. Start by letting your community know what you are doing for it and how you're helping. And seek visibility or popularity through traditional media outlets, and more alternative ones (i.e., TED Talks, social media).

Above all else, learn how to tell your story in the most compelling way. Look at how successfully Jobs, Musk, Jack Ma or Branson were able to do this. This grew their reputations to the point where they became better known than their products. And it allowed them to become legend.

Musk: The disrupting innovator—"Failure is an option here. If things are not failing, you are not innovating enough."

Branson: The social capitalist—"The way you treat your employees is the way they will treat your customers."

Jobs: The genius—"I want to put a ding in the universe."

Jack Ma: The regular guy who failed many times—"When KFC came to China, 24 people went for the job, 23 people were accepted. I was the only guy."

Chapter 5

BONUS CHAPTER

Miscellaneous of tools that have proved useful in startups:

- Three moves ahead rule
- Funds
- Internal versus external resources: how to run lean and mean
- Startup golden metric: perceived value + user satisfaction
- The future four battlefields for startups

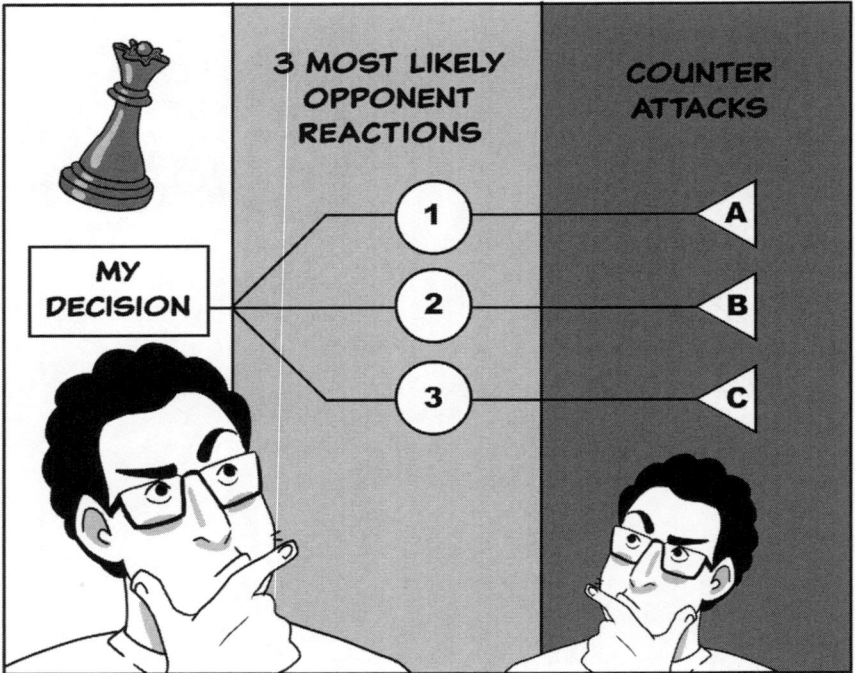

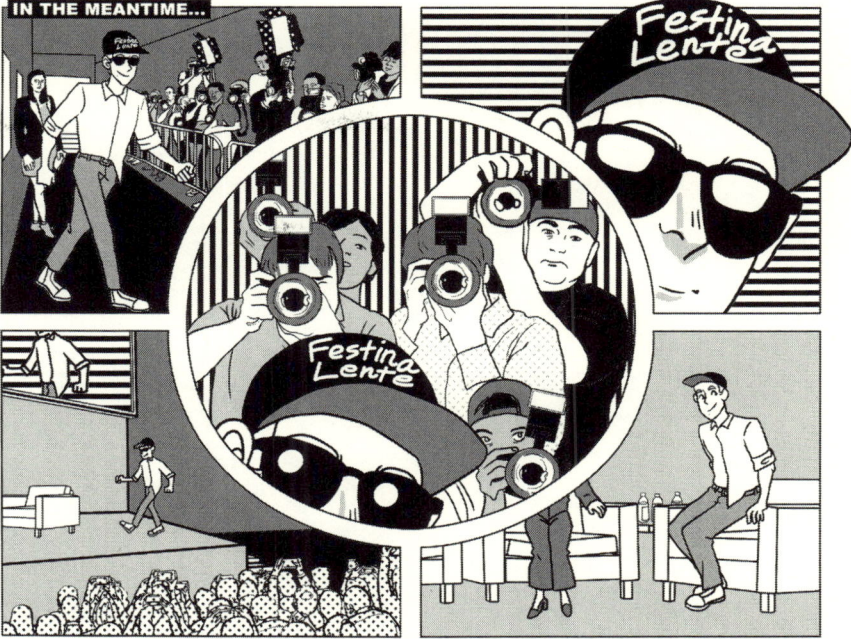

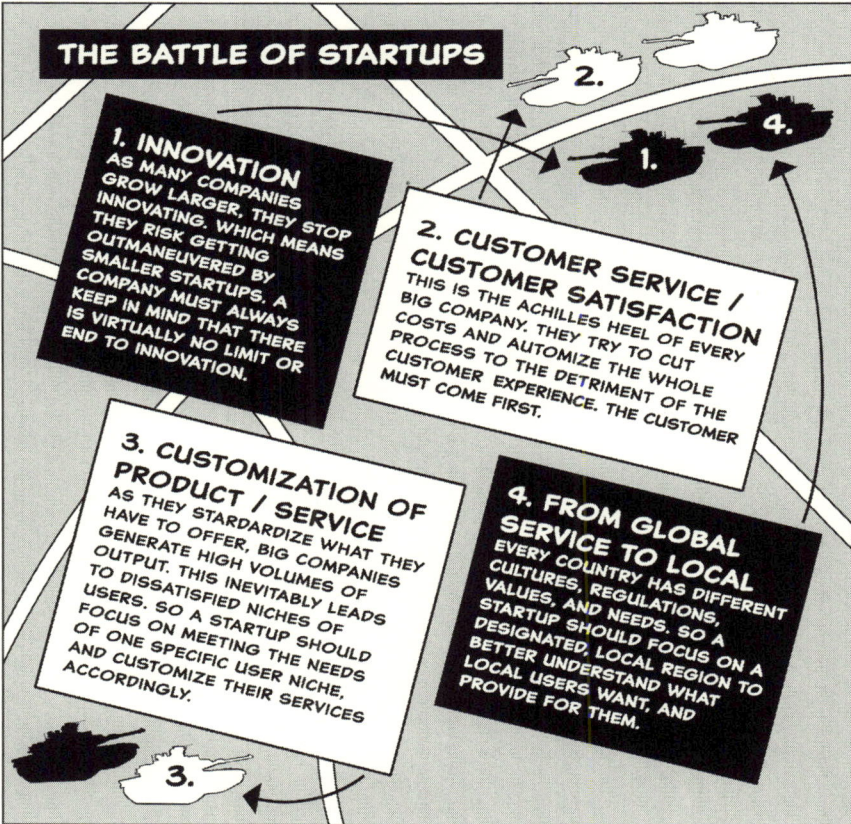

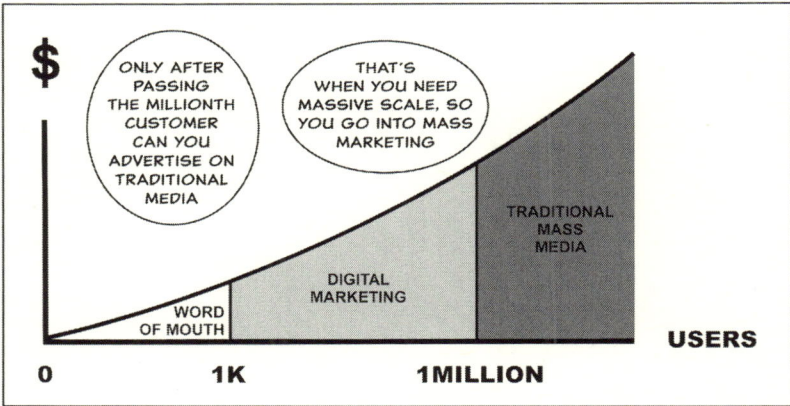

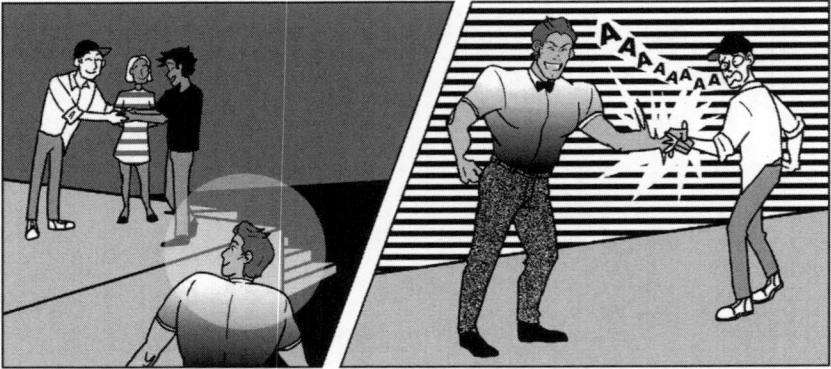

WHICH IS WHY WE NEED TO POINT OUT A MARKET NEED

ASTONISHINGLY, 42% OF STARTUPS FAIL BECAUSE THERE IS NO MARKET NEED FOR THE PRODUCT OR SERVICE THEY OFFER

IN OTHER WORDS, YOU CAN HAVE A GREAT PRODUCT WITH REVOLUTIONARY TECHNOLOGY,

BUT IF IT'S NOT USEFUL FOR END USERS, IT WILL BE A FIASCO

SO HOW DO YOU MEASURE IF YOUR STARTUP HAS A VALID PRODUCT OR SERVICE?

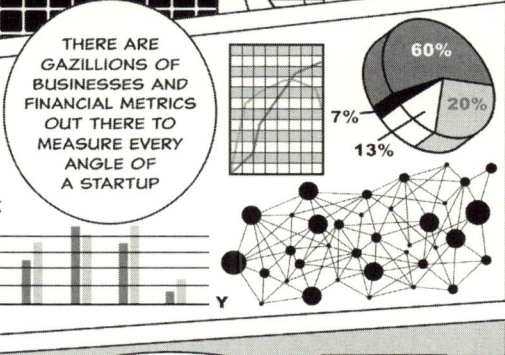

THERE ARE GAZILLIONS OF BUSINESSES AND FINANCIAL METRICS OUT THERE TO MEASURE EVERY ANGLE OF A STARTUP

HOWEVER, THE TWO MOST SIGNIFICANT THINGS TO MEASURE, ESPECIALLY AT THE EARLY STAGES, ARE PERCEIVED USEFULNESS AND USER SATISFACTION

MANY FOUNDERS AND VCS OVERLOOK THESE,

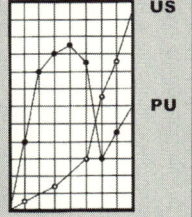

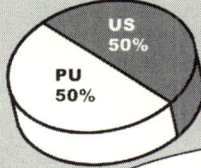

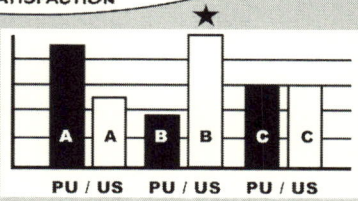

WHICH IS WHY WE SEE SO MANY NEW APPS AND BUSINESSES THAT TYPICALLY ARE NOT SOLVING ANY USERS' PROBLEMS

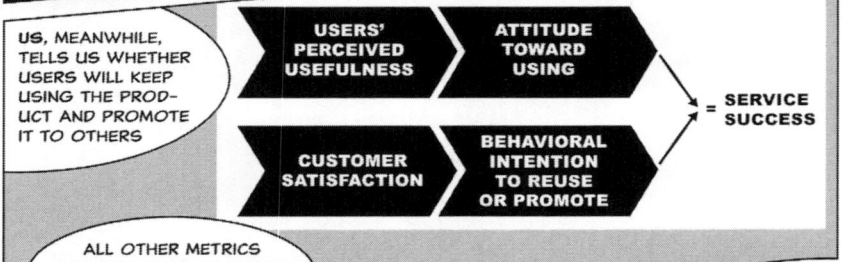

Bonus Chapter

Raising Funds

Funds are the lifeblood of a startup and must start flowing quickly. A founder otherwise risks losing time and grip as the team morale may be negatively affected and ultimately the startup survival may be compromised.

At first, personal funds are the most viable way to validate your ideas and to build a prototype. To complement personal funds, look to the three Fs: Family, Friends and Fools.

Crowdfunding platforms such as Kickstarter and Indiegogo can be a valuable tool for raising initial capital.

When you're looking for funding from VCs, Angels or whomever, presenting a prototype is absolutely critical. Don't just give them an abstracted idea or another boring PowerPoint presentation. A prototype makes your vision tangible.

Even better—try to have some users test your prototype to prove that it works. This will help you gain credibility, and will dramatically increase your chances of getting the big bucks.

In order to keep growing, you should eventually transition from personal funds to Venture Capital. Some startups are able to sustain its growth organically using cash flow. A successful example of such organic growth is represented by Mailchimp.

Mailchimp didn't skyrocket to success overnight; it's been around since 2001. Initially, it didn't raise huge amounts of venture capital, nor did it have a big sales team. But its small team spent years experimenting, testing and creating a functional product that now serves millions of people around the world. Sixteen years after its founding, Mailchimp reached $400 million in revenue with just 550 employees.

This goes to show that however essential funds are, they can't alone buy success of a startup.

It's never a single ingredient that makes a delicious dish, but a balanced mixture of them. As discussed in previous chapters and seen with Mailchimp, a startup needs a strong and motivated team, an innovative or disruptive idea, good technology and the willingness to test itself and evolve. No amount of money will otherwise suffice to keep it afloat.

The Three Elements

As we've seen, some startups find success by filling market gaps. However, most find themselves competing with small-/medium-sized startups that offer similar services, and they face the problem of getting users to switch from the old to the new.

Pushing people to change is always difficult, as it causes a great deal of discomfort. In a competitive market, how then can a new startup facilitate this transition and make an impact?

Three elements are key:

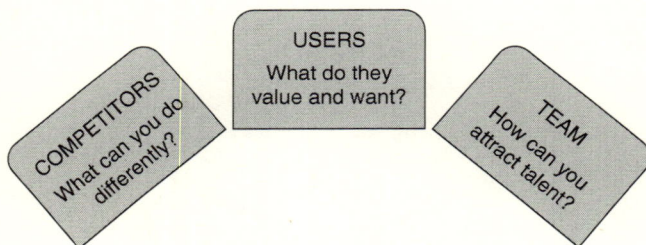

USERS
What do they
value and want?

COMPETITORS
What can you do
differently?

TEAM
How can you
attract talent?

Element 1: Competitors

You must be your competitor's first and biggest user. Learn from them and improve upon their mistakes. Often, established companies get complacent and fail to innovate. This means they lose sight of their users, and their users' evolving needs.

23andMe versus MyHeritage: 23andMe was founded in 2006 by Linda Avey, Paul Cusenza and Anne Wojcicki, ex-wife of Google cofounder Sergey Brin. It's one of the biggest companies in DNA mapping service kits with over 2 million customers in the United States. However, when it was first launched, it had two key weaknesses:

First, when you received the kit, you had to fill an entire sample cup with your saliva within 30 minutes, which wasn't a pleasant experience for users.

Second, it provided result only in English, which meant it lost the opportunity to build a larger DNA database within a much larger market.

MyHeritage took advantage of these weakness. It made the saliva collection process much less painless by requiring only a quick swab of your cheek. It also offered the service in 42 different languages. It proceeded to build one of the largest international networks of family trees with over 8.8 billion historical records and 92 million users, becoming the number one provider of DNA kits.

Element 2: Users

Users are constantly evolving. That means there are endless opportunities to create services that satisfy them. Users also tend to get bored, and usually they get excited about innovative things. Early startups are therefore encouraged to test their ideas on small batches of them. Once they validate their idea, they should target **dissatisfied users** and **early adopters** in order to gain initial traction. Look for reviews on blogs and in magazines by influencers and evangelists. Such reviews are invaluable as they will not pass unnoticed.

Element 3: Team

Great talents are always looking for new adventures, or simply to find their one true passion. Many can be found in corporate entities bored and waiting for the opportunity to shine. You can be the one to give them that opportunity. So always think about what your startup represents, and what it can mean for the market, and the world.

Measuring Your Startup

How can you measure the potential success of your startup? There are tons of valid marketing and financial metrics out there, and all of them are somewhat useful. That said, the most relevant metrics, which form an umbrella over the rest, are **Perceived Usefulness (PU)** and **User Satisfaction (US)**.

PU: The users' willingness to try the product/service.
US: Whether users will keep using the product/service and recommend it to others.

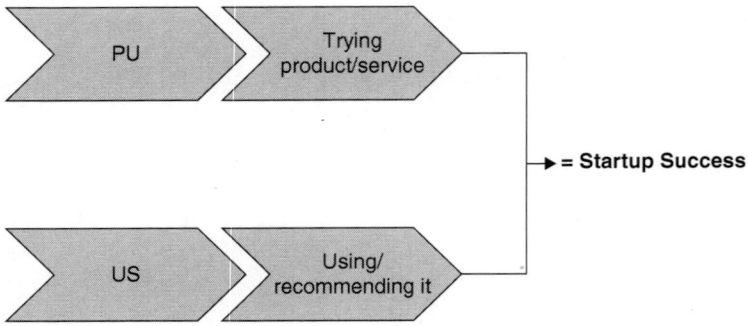

Many founders and investors overlook these two measurements, still thinking, "If you build it they will come." That's why we see so many new apps and businesses that don't solve any problems or offer anything particularly novel.

Astonishingly, the main reason for a startup's failure (42 percent) is that there's no market need for that product/service. In other words, you can have a great product with revolutionary technology, but if it's not perceived as useful by the end users, it will be a sure fiasco.

Internal versus External Resources

Small startups have limited resources and capabilities and they need to run lean and mean. So when should you outsource without compromising the value of your product or service?

Everything that is part of your core competencies—in other words, your know-how—should be done internally, whether this means marketing, programming, PR, networking, and so on. The rest should be outsourced. The smaller you are, the more you should outsource. So,

DO outsource everything cyclical such as taxes, accounting and legal services.
DO outsource everything that can be standardized within your startup, such as customer service or administrative tasks.
DON'T outsource what makes you different.
DON'T outsource your strengths.
DON'T outsource your unique know-how.

A rule of thumb for startups is to outsource 80 percent and keep 20 percent in-house.

Technically, you could outsource everything to free up resources and run faster. But outsourcing too much will weaken your startup and likely decrease the value of your service or product.

An interesting case of too much outsourcing can be seen in **Hello Alfred**, the personal concierge startup founded by two Harvard grads.

Through the Hello Alfred app, you can book someone to run your errands, such as buying groceries, cleaning your apartment, going to the post office, etc. On its website, Hello Alfred advertises its butlers, or "Alfreds," as spirited go-getters willing to do almost anything for a client—as long as it's legal.

Sounds ideal for chaotic city dwellers whose every moment is precious, right? However, despite investors pouring millions of dollars into the startup, it never really took off. The founders tried hard to promote it in the NYC subway, using colorful and fun billboards. They even teamed up with important companies such as Related Real Estate to promote Hello Alfred to building tenants. Still, the service floundered and its expansion was thwarted.

The secret problem with Hello Alfred is that it outsourced all of its tasks to third parties. There are two tiers of service: $32 per week gets you one visit, and $59 gets you two visits. Otherwise, it uses Instacart to buy groceries, MyClean to clean apartments, and Uber as a carrier.

By outsourcing all these adds-on, the user ends up paying a fortune, and the value of the "Alfreds" are proportionally diminished.

Another case of too much of outsourcing occurred to Dell Computer.

Dell Computer hit its stride in the 1990s and quickly became one of the most successful and profitable computer companies in the world. But over time, in an attempt to continually improve its efficiency metrics and financial ratios such as RONA, the company outsourced many of its operations to a Taiwanese company, called ASUS. Profitability skyrocketed and Dell analysts rewarded the company accordingly. The data on Dell's balance sheet looked good. But the phenomena behind the data—the innovative prowess of the company—didn't. In 2005, after Dell had outsourced enough activities to ASUS—effectively putting the company into business—ASUS announced the creation of its own brand of computer. And the rest, as they say, became history.

By outsourcing its know-how, Dell diminished its value offer and strengthen its supplier to the point it became its competitor.

Bridging the Experience Gap

By definition, startups are innovative organizations. This means you'll inevitably find yourself attempting to solve problems in fields in which you're not an expert. Additionally, you'll have to make difficult decisions without decades of relevant experience under your belt. That said, there are ways to mitigate these problems and navigate these tough situations.

(1) Surround yourself with advisors or mentors.
(2) Constantly ask questions.
(3) Keep training and educating your team.
(4) Test all of your hypotheses with real users.
(5) Create a library of startup successes and failures. Read case studies and stories. Learn about winning strategies, find analogies and correlations and observe the remarkable actions of other leaders. See how they solved similarly tough problems.

There will be times when it's necessary to work 20-hour shifts. But there will also be slow times, which you should use wisely. Make sure you do plenty of research on your own, and play a few games with your team as well, such as:

- The **3 Moves Ahead Game**: Try to come up with relevant scenarios and their potential outcomes. This will not only help you brainstorm the best new strategies but will also prepare you for difficult situations (see Chapter 4). For example, ask yourselves: if we make our app free for six months, how will users react? How about competitors? If they match our strategy, how will we differentiate?
- The **"What-If Scenarios" Game**: Simulate an emergency plan if something goes wrong. Or do some stress tests to discover weaknesses. I played this game when mentoring one particular startup, and not surprisingly, the founders discovered many weaknesses that they'd not previously considered. For example, they realized they didn't have a backup plan for their archives in case of a system crash.

The bottom line: it's always a good idea to fix the roof on a sunny day.

The User Is King

It will always be hard for small startups to compete with the giants in terms of prices, features, etc. But as we've discussed, a small startup should choose its battles wisely—battles it can win. Such as customer service.

Big companies serve huge amounts of clients, which means they likely disappoint or overlook a good portion of them. How many times have you found yourself shouting at an automated voice message? In addition, they don't always put the customer first, but instead look to maximize the shareholders' value, as is the goal of public companies.

Startups should use this to their advantage and focus on something else, something far more important: to maximize value for its users. For example, add a personal touch to your service. Have users talk to an actual human.

Think in terms of R&D efforts. Recently, big oil and gas companies found an innovative way to pump oil horizontally in order to exploit reservoirs that had previously been inaccessible. However, this breakthrough did nothing to help end users filling up their gas tanks.

And think about that trendy new restaurant you used to love. It managed to break into the highly competitive market by offering you the best quality ingredients. But once it won you and other foodies over, rather than innovating its menu by adding seasonal dishes, hoping to win over even more customers, they started using frozen ingredients to cut costs.

Startups must always focus on delivering value and constantly reinvesting their profits to serve this goal.

Reinvesting your profits in customer satisfaction is far better than spending them on ads or marketing campaigns. Word of mouth is still the most powerful weapon.

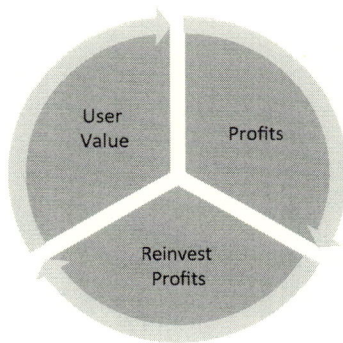

User Value➜Profits➜Reinvest profits (training employees, reduced pain points of your service, R&D, etc.)➜ User Value➜ Profits

ACKNOWLEDGMENTS

I wanted to start by thanking everyone who believed in *The Art of Startups* when it was nothing more than an idea. Christopher Impiglia, friend and editor of the book, thank you for your time, expertise and for always being there from day one. I'm incredibly grateful to Sakura Maku and Daniela Coca as well, both for their beautiful art and their ability to interpret my writing so perfectly. I must also thank them for their patience during the numerous rounds of revisions. Working with them has been a pleasure.

Thanks to Mohar Chakrabarty for his mentoring, friendship and generosity, as well as to the 129 literary agents who turned this project down because it was too "innovative" or "risky." Their rejections led me to the best publisher I could ever wish for. Tej Sood, my publisher, thank you for your enthusiasm from the moment you saw this book, and for wanting to make it happen. Thanks to Abi, Megan, Kyra and the rest of the Anthem Press team for their support and their work to make this book tangible.

Thanks to the *Financial Times* and McKinsey & Co. and the Bracken Bower Prize, specifically to Andrew Hill and Michael Birshan. Having this book chosen in the top 12 business book proposals of 2018 gave me invaluable exposure and momentum as a new author. It also allowed me to meet numerous talented voices from around the world.

Thanks to Prof. Susanna Gallani, Prof. Robert Kaplan, Prof. Dennis Campbell and Prof. Robert Simons of Harvard Business School, and to Prof. Larry Bridwell at Pace University for all their input and insight.

Thanks to ThyssenKrupp, especially to the engineer Tre Watts of the Research Innovation Center, and to the mechanic Stanley Ksiazek for their support in developing innovative solutions.

Thanks to Gianluca Giansante for his advising and coaching.

Thanks to Marco Magnani for reminding me that there are no secrets or shortcuts in making a good book, just discipline, time and hard work.

Thanks to Joe Gebbia for the passion he puts into everything he does.

Thanks to all of the startuppers and entrepreneurs whom I have met along the way. Their stories are continuous sources of inspiration.

Finally, thank you to my wife, Julia, for her invaluable help, support and infinite patience throughout all the book development.

Edoardo Maggini is a serial entrepreneur who has co-founded three startup companies within the last decade alone. He worked for several years in New York for a Fortune 500 company as operations manager. Edoardo, is currently working at his startup company, Fenix Technologies, in the cleantech industry. In his spare time, he coaches and mentor startup founders. Edoardo studied at Pace University and at Harvard Business School.